"*Let There Be Science* provides fascinating new science and faith. Full of engaging examples, th informs, and challenges, breathing new life in historical roots."

Denis Alexander, Emeritus Director of The Faraday Institute for Science and Religion, St. Edmund's College, Cambridge

"A fascinating and highly original contribution to the God and science discussion. David and Tom show that rather than science and Christianity being at war with each other, there's a powerful fit between science and faith. Far from Christianity only being for Dawkins's 'dyed-in-the-wool faith heads', *Let There Be Science* lays out a myriad ways that Christianity offers rich resources for science – including the most powerful motive for doing science in the first place."

Dr Andy Bannister, Director of the Solas Centre for Public Christianity, Adjunct Speaker, Ravi Zacharias International Ministries

"This book is a highly thought-provoking exploration of the relationship between science and faith. The authors' arguments are clearly and elegantly presented, and supported with fascinating examples from the history of the exploration of science. Recommended for non-scientists and scientists alike, it is a surprising and unexpected page-turner."

Angie Edwards, Director of the Arthur C. Clarke Foundation

"How do scientists interact with the cosmos as God's creation? Here is an unexpected interlacing of fascinating science stories with an even larger framework of Biblical understanding. A really thoughtful and wide-ranging encounter."

Owen Gingerich, Professor emeritus of Astronomy and History of Science, Harvard-Smithsonian Center for Astrophysics

"Whatever your personal stance on matters of religion and science, it's surely encouraging to see calm and considered conversation being fostered between them. *Let There Be Science* makes a compelling case that the ethos of science and the insights that it brings into the workings of the natural world can have much to offer to people of faith. With passion and humility David Hutchings and Tom McLeish seek out common ground and show that, despite our differences, we are all united in our curiosity and capacity for wonder."

Dr Marek Kukula, Public Astronomer, Royal Observatory Greenwich

"An immensely enjoyable and readable account of some of the big questions raised by modern science. The authors provide a wealth of detail as they open up their exciting vision of the relationship of science and Christian faith. Highly recommended."

Alister McGrath, Andreas Idreos Professor of Science and Religion, Oxford University

"This is a brilliant book which uses fascinating human stories to demonstrate how science and religion belong together in the exploration of fundamental questions about life and the nature of reality. In an easy, approachable style the authors take us into the Big Ideas of science and shine on them the enriching light of biblical wisdom. It's a thrilling journey and renews the reader's hope for a mature partnership between the great world views of science and religion, whereby each is a gift to the other and all of us are the beneficiaries. Read, mark, and enjoy."

The Rt Revd John Pritchard, former Bishop of Oxford

"*Let There Be Science* is engagingly written so as to be thought-provoking to both the sceptic and evangelist alike. The book tackles prejudices and stereotypes head-on with such honesty that its effect is to engage and gently challenge rather than to patronise or preach. Whatever your persuasion you are likely to learn and be engaged with some beautiful science and find yourself grappling with the complexities of our human condition – including our fascination with religion. A stimulating and highly enjoyable read."

Professor Sarah Thompson MBE, FInstP, Head of Department of Physics, University of York, Vice President Institute of Physics (Science and Innovation)

"At a time when one of the great fallacies of our age continues to suggest that science and theology are incompatible, Tom McLeish and David Hutchings bring a creative dialogue between the two disciplines in *Let There Be Science*. They present a compelling vision, describing science as a gift from God in which science and theology interrelate and thrive in each other's company. A timely book which shows Christian apologetics and the public understanding of science at its very best."

The Rt Revd Graham Usher, Bishop of Dudley

"This is a book about the wonderfully human nature of science by two most wonderfully human of authors. A must read for those who fear or dismiss science and for those who make science into an idol. Here is the reality of science in all of its fun, its success, its complexity, its limitations, and its relationship to faith."

Revd Professor David Wilkinson, Principal of St John's College and Professor in the Department of Theology and Religion, Durham University

SCIENCE

WHY GOD LOVES SCIENCE, AND SCIENCE NEEDS GOD

David Hutchings and Tom McLeish

LION

For the glory of God: Father, Son, and Holy Spirit.

Published by Lion Books
an imprint of
Lion Hudson plc
Wilkinson House, Jordan Hill Road,
Oxford OX2 8DR, England
www.lionhudson.com/lion

ISBN 978 0 7459 6863 6
e-ISBN 978 0 7459 6864 3

First edition 2017

Acknowledgments
Scripture quotations taken from the Holy Bible, New International Version
Anglicised. Copyright © 1979, 1984, 2011 Biblica, formerly International
Bible Society. Used by permission of Hodder & Stoughton Ltd, an Hachette UK
company. All rights reserved. "NIV" is a registered trademark of Biblica. UK
trademark number 1448790.

p. 38: Extract from Gregory of Nyssa, *On the Soul and the Resurrection* © 1993 tr.
C. P. Roth, reprinted by permission of St Vladimir's Seminary Press.
pp. 61, 62: Extracts from *Monty Python and the Holy Grail* © 1975 Python
(Monty) Pictures Limited, used by permission.
p. 110: Extracts from *Rosencrantz and Guildenstern are Dead* © 1967 Faber and
Faber, used by permission.
p. 132: Extracts from Andre Geim in the original full length Nobel Lecture from
nobelprize.org © 2010 The Nobel Foundation, used by permission.
pp. 159, 160: Extracts from *Genesis in Space and Time* © 1975 Francis Schaeffer,
reprinted by permission of IVP.

Cover images: All istockphoto.com – silhouette © dan-belitsky; high voltage
strike © tolokonov; lens flare © skegbydave; digital lens flare © Mr_POKPAK.

A catalogue record for this book is available from the British Library

Printed and bound in the UK, December 2016, LH36

CONTENTS

FOREWORD

"I wonder as I wander out under the sky"

So begins one of the best-loved Christmas carols. *Wonder.* It is the beginning of both science and the Christian faith. Wonder that the world is as it is, in its beauty, majesty, and glory. Wonder also that "God so loved the world that he gave his only Son, so that everyone who believes in him may not perish but may have eternal life."[1]

Wonder like this can only find expression in praise. As the biblical Psalmist writes, "I praise you, for I am fearfully and wonderfully made. Wonderful are your works; that I know very well."[2] We are indeed wonder-fully made – God has made us to be full of wonder for both him and his works.

Just as Augustine says that "God has made us for himself, and our hearts are restless until they find their rest in him,"[3] God has also made us for this world, and our minds are restless until they find their rest in its truth. For, as we explore and discover more about the world, we come to know more about God's wonder-full works, and so come to know God himself more and more. Thus, in doing science – in seeking the truth about the world around us – we worship God.

And this, then, is why faith provides such a natural environment for science to flourish – as the authors of this book maintain. They show, through stories about faith and science, that rather than faith being the enemy of science (as many of the "cultured despisers" would have us believe) faith *nurtures* science, watering its roots so that it may bear fruit; fruit that will last.

Now, this fruit isn't merely the satisfying of curiosity – the scratching of an intellectual itch – but rather, just as faith leads to action, so does science. God has given us the gift of science, and the gift of faith to nurture it, so that we may actively engage the world, making it a better place not only for ourselves but also for those who come after us. This is part of what it means to be human; and science, along with and supported by faith, is right at the heart of it.

I commend this book to all who would like to know better how faith is fertile ground for the growth of science. But in closing, I would like to say more generally that faith is an environment not only where science thrives, but also where human life thrives. We are all pilgrims, wandering in this world. There will be a time, however, when our pilgrimages come to an end: in that place of joy which "no eye has seen, nor ear heard, nor the human heart conceived, what God has prepared for those who love him."[4] And there, all our wanderings will cease – for, though "we know now only in part, there we will know fully, even as we have been fully known."[5] And, in turn, science will come to an end; for not only will we know the mind of God, we will see him face to face.

The Archbishop of York, Dr John Sentamu

PREFACE

Dave

The whole thing is almost depressingly predictable. Each school year, the students I teach find out that I believe in God – either because they have asked me outright or because it has turned up in conversation somehow. From then, I can count it down:

3... 2... 1...

"But you're a *science* teacher!"

It isn't their fault, of course. Somehow, even before their mid-teens, they think that you just have to pick a side – God or science. Who has told them this? Science-hating God-people? God-hating scientists?

Either way, it doesn't take long to establish that there hasn't been much real thought involved in their forming of the "it's either God or science" conclusion – it has just sort of happened. A few simple questions expose the truth that they have ended up believing it without really knowing why. I suspect that it is because someone, somewhere, has been doing the media-based equivalent of shouting aggressively at whoever happens to be nearby – and that my students, like everyone else, have picked up the echoes and settled for that.

What might happen, though, if we stopped with all the shouting? What if we just talked, and listened? Might Bible-believing Christians have something to say to scientists that is not just interesting, but actually beneficial to real-world science? Might scientists have something to say to Christians that could help them live out their day-to-day faith more powerfully?

Even in those questions, we see a false split, for there is no need for an individual to be one or the other. There are many scientists who are also committed Christians. The shouters, of course, don't want people to know this, and especially not to think about it; which is precisely why they shout. The problem, however, is that it is a fact, and facts are powerful things – they need to be dealt with.

Yet how can this be done, and done well? The temptation is to join in as loudly as others have – but that is only really likely to make things worse. Shouting sets people up against each other and breaks down both conversation and thought. A handful of teachers encouraging a handful of students to think the God-science issue through more carefully might make a small difference, but it certainly won't bring about wholescale change.

Is there, maybe, a way that we can let all the echoes die down slightly and start afresh? Can we give everyone – students, scientists, priests and pastors, and none of the above – a new beginning? Might they be gifted the chance to start thinking, in an environment that permits even the gentler voices to be heard, about how God and science relate to each other?

It was with questions like these working their way around my head that I found myself, a few years ago, listening to a lecture on Astrophysics. The talk – "Black Holes, White Holes and Worm Holes" was expertly delivered by Dame Jocelyn Bell Burnell, a legendary figure in physics, known best for her discovery of pulsars. Had justice been done, in fact, she would have a Nobel Prize for it – but, as we will go on to see in this book, the world of science yields up just as many failures and missteps as any other. It was at this lecture's after-party (yes, there really was one) that I first met Professor Tom McLeish.

I had just been having a discussion with Dame Jocelyn about God – thankfully, she is most certainly not a shouter – so my mind was already on such things when Tom walked over and mentioned a book he had just written. It was about Christianity and science, he said. I find myself thinking of this as a divine encounter of some sort – I bought a copy and, in the ensuing months, some wonderful answers to my wonderings about fresh starts began to emerge. To see why, and to get a little more background, it only seems fair to hand over to Tom himself...

Tom

For several years, this scientist and Christian had, like Dave, become increasingly frustrated at the amount of defensive writing in "science and religion". The ever-present, "How can you reconcile the conflict between science and faith?" seemed to start from the wrong place, and assume all the wrong things. I wanted very much to think out loud more about questions that went along the lines, "What is science for in God's great project?"

Implied in this "science within Christian belief" approach were two other necessary things. We would need to listen to the great thinkers about the natural world throughout history, especially those whose love of the natural world evidently sprang from their faith. Excitingly for science, this "long view" also shows that it is much more deeply human than the "science is modern" view that I had been sold as a student. It also meant a fresh approach to the Bible. While the book of Genesis is a wonderful document about God's creation and covenant, it dawned on me that it doesn't contain the Bible's simplest creation stories, nor the most important material on how to think about nature. That seemed to be in the less well known (and much less talked about) "Wisdom" books. Special among them is the even less-well-read Book of Job, whose probing celebration of the natural world

I love. That all lead to the book, Faith and Wisdom in Science *– the one Dave went and read.*

I wrote that first book with a graduate reader in mind – its language comes from the university world I inhabit and work in day to day. But the message and ideas – that we can think Biblically about science as God's gift, as a talent to turn into many-fold returns as the world, and that this can transform the way we think about science – can be chewed-on by anyone. In particular I had realised that Faith and Wisdom in Science *had serious consequences for education and the media. Andrew Hodder-Williams from Lion Hudson (incidentally an old school friend) had approached me about writing for a wider readership, including those of any age who may not have studied or embraced either science or faith in any meaningful way. I just didn't think I would be able to do it very well. I needed a co-author. If only I could find, say, a school science teacher with a gift for writing and who shared my passion for science within God's Kingdom...*

Dave and Tom

The result of this, hopefully, is a book about what we might be able to hear underneath all of the shouting. It is a book about what Christianity says about science, and about what science says about Christianity – all through stories of interest to readers of all faiths or none. It seeks to pick up on what has, all too often, been drowned out by the noise: that science flows naturally from the Christian worldview, and that it always has.

How sad it is that this extraordinary relationship has been almost completely lost in inaccurate or over-emphasised tales of the prejudices, mistakes, and terrible deeds that have sometimes arisen in the name of either faith or science. For every disaster, there are a multitude of remarkable success stories, nearly all of which seem never to be told.

It is time, now, for this to be remedied. The Bible's message speaks of a God who loves science and of a science that needs God. Again and again, this has been proved to be true in the real world of physics, chemistry, and biology. This is a book about those instances and the wonderful message which is threaded through each of them: that science is a gift from God, one with unlimited potential for good, and we are all to treasure it greatly, whether experts or not.

Great things can happen in relationships whenever people are prepared to stop shouting. Maybe, one day, things could be different in classrooms, laboratories, churches, and pubs. Perhaps we can become a society that thinks and talks about facts, and not just echoes. That the Big Picture of Christianity and the practice of modern science weave together beautifully is, putting it simply, true.

So, let's seek out these two – science and faith – in all of their fullness, and rediscover that beauty ourselves.

Tom

I'd like to thank Dave for taking this project on and for writing mostly everything (the reader should know this). We'd both like to thank Andrew Hodder-Williams, Jessica Scott, and especially Becki Bradshaw at Lion for their encouragement and hard work. The most loving supporters of projects like this as well as the most sensitive critics are the close family who also have to put up with it; without all that from my wife Julie and our children this wouldn't have happened.

Dave

Since I have never really done anything like this before, I have very many people to thank. Tom, Becki and Andrew have, I feel, taken a risk in working with a newbie like me, and I am hugely grateful for that. Their advice and patience has been much needed. My wife, Emma, has taken much of the brunt of the book – having to read countless excerpts, put up with my absence, listen to my ramblings and humour me almost constantly. She has done this whilst also looking after a toddler (Bethany) and a baby (Chloe), although they have probably caused her fewer difficulties than I have. I couldn't have done any of this without her.

Others who have helped with the manuscript in significant ways are Joshua Crosby, Becki Dean, Ed Hambleton, and Liam Maxwell. Their feedback has been vital in producing what we have all now ended up with. Colleagues at Pocklington School have also been key aids; they shall have to be satisfied with being listed by their initials: IHA, MJA, MJD, AWJH, GJH and LAL. I promised to mention one of my Physics A Level classes, L6Q, who were refreshingly honest with me about whether what I was writing was even remotely interesting. (In return, may I remind them now, they have promised to buy a copy each). Of course, I also owe a huge debt to my parents, in particular for their constant encouragement and prayers. Finally, Lawrence Osborn – our copy editor – was both flexible with timings and wise in his analysis of the text. Thank you to all.

Thank you

1

TURNING THE LIGHT ON

He who walks in the darkness does not know where he is going.

Jesus of Nazareth

Shin: a device for finding furniture in the dark.

Steven Wright

Finding the best path across an unlit and cluttered room in the middle of the night is a potentially tricky business. The horrors of a stubbed toe or of treading on something sharp are only ever one unlucky step away. The solution is obvious, of course, provided it is available: turn the light on. The newly illuminated surroundings can now be taken in – plotting a course is made much easier.

Writing something new about science feels a little bit like this crowded-room scenario, especially since this book will deal with some controversial subject matter. What exactly, we shall ask, *is* science? What is science *for*? Do these questions, interesting though they might be, really make any practical difference? Would knowing the answers actually change anything for the average scientist?

Unsurprisingly, the room these questions occupy is a hazardous one. It is already stuffed full of furniture, and there are oddments all over its floor. Stepping out into it will mean putting feet and shins at serious risk – and only more so if we allow the ideas and language of *faith* to have any involvement.

A thoughtful and careful look at the big-picture story of science, though, shows that the topic of faith is simply unavoidable; it crops up again and again. In fact, at times, faith appears not just to be part of the mix, but central to it. Although this might seem unexpected at first, a bit more exploration reveals what is at least a partial explanation: science – so often presented as a detached, almost robotic undertaking – turns out in reality to be startlingly, and wonderfully, *human*.

When it comes to real-world science, as we shall see, it is no exaggeration at all to say that personality (with its worldviews, instincts, and quirks) has made at least as much difference as rationality. Throughout history, religious beliefs have consistently informed – and sometimes even brought about – new and successful scientific theories. The Christian faith, in particular, seems to be able to provide an environment in which science can positively thrive. If we are serious about answering the big questions laid out above, we cannot really afford to ignore these considerations – on the contrary, we should investigate them further.

As we do so, we will discover that there are many good reasons for the positive effects of faith on scientific endeavour. Chief among these is the provision of a powerful underlying *reason* for doing science in the first place – one that is so powerful that it is unparalleled anywhere else in human thought. This key principle of purpose has led to Christianity being intimately involved with – in some cases being directly responsible for – many of the biggest leaps forward in scientific history.

Maybe, then, it is not actually all that unscientific to hear faith speak as we seek to evaluate and then support science – it could prove to be a more useful travelling companion than some might have thought. Perhaps our seemingly inbuilt love of wisdom about nature really does have some sort of ultimate, faith-related significance. Can Christianity – and its key text, the Bible – help us, in some tangible way, to understand science better? Can it speak on what science *is*? Can it speak on what it is *for*?

Before we start answering these questions, however, it might be wise to ask one more: what ideas are already out there about science? After all, many voices have spoken out about its role or its value or its relationship with human beings, and it would be wise to hear these first. In this opening chapter, therefore, we will do just that.

Let us think of this initial listening process as turning the light on and surveying the room. For only once we have done so, will we be ready to plan out our route; a route which will – if it is the right one – bring us safely to a better place.

Science, Faith, and Hard Words

There is little doubt that the word "science" seems to come with strong images and ideas attached to it. Parents' evenings at schools are full of surprised mums and dads declaring that they "never really *got* science" after being told their offspring is doing quite well in physics. There is the definite notion that some (odd) people are just "good at science" – unlike the rest of those mere mortals who will work in "normal" areas like retail, manufacturing, the leisure industry, or some form of office work.

Ask people to associate words with "science" and their responses reinforce this idea: "difficult", "boring", "mad scientist" all crop up. This does not necessarily mean that science is unvalued, though, since other answers are "experiment", "proof", and "curing cancer". Instead, it seems that science is viewed as useful, but complicated. Is this true about other complex human activities? What if we try the same process with "music" or "art"?

This time, answers are far more *personal*. They might be a favourite song or a feeling – there is far less sense of distance or threat. When most people talk about science, they do so from a position of wariness – it is part of a different world that they feel they can comment *on* but not really take part *in* – and yet other subjects are seen as more comfortable and accessible. We could, therefore, call science a "hard" idea, and these others "soft".

What about our other key topic, faith? Is it hard or soft? Words like "trust", and "belief" sound somewhat promising, but do not push faith clearly into one category or the other. Expressions like "blind faith" and "extremism", however, are certainly nearer the hard end of the spectrum.

When considering the interaction of faith and science, then, we might be entering grounds in which people have strong ideas, even if they don't have a high level of personal involvement in either area. The atmosphere in which the two meet could be highly charged at times, and this book finds itself right in the middle of it – so paying attention to what has been said before will be very important.

It is perhaps most obvious to start with the scientist most often associated with this meeting-point, Richard Dawkins. He is quoted often, partially because he is so strongly spoken. Take, for instance, his comments during a live webchat on the *mumsnet* website:

> If children understand that beliefs should be substantiated with evidence, as opposed to tradition, authority, revelation or faith, they will automatically work out for themselves that they are atheists.[1]

It is a relatively simple point: *evidence* (which comes from doing science) is *opposed* to *faith* (which, according to Dawkins, contains no evidence) and leads to the obvious conclusion (since a child can arrive at it) that there is no God. For Dawkins, science and faith are enemies, and science must win out in the world for us to progress. He is far from being alone in this view, with the more active supporters of it being dubbed the "New Atheists". Peter Atkins, a former professor of chemistry at Oxford University, is unafraid of adding his voice to Dawkins':

> It is not possible to be intellectually honest and believe in gods. And it is not possible to believe in gods and be a true scientist.[2]

These bold announcements, however, have been challenged by the very creatures that Peter Atkins does not believe exist: true scientists who do believe. Alister McGrath, himself a professor at Oxford, is both a biophysicist and a theologian. As a former atheist, he writes that the evidence for God can be found repeatedly within science:

> The Christian faith... allows us to see further and deeper, to appreciate that nature is studded with signs, radiant with reminders, and emblazoned with symbols of God, our creator and redeemer.[3]

Such back-and-forth between supposed enemies has generated hundreds of books, YouTube videos, podcasts, and university debates. Some titles give a sense of the discussion: *The God Delusion*, *The Dawkins Delusion*, *Faith vs. Fact*, *Gunning for God: why the New Atheists are Missing the Target*, and so on. Each new publication seeks to build the case further for either the death or the defence of faith, with science being hauled in to flesh out the argument.

As a side-effect, all this has led to a fear of science among some religious communities. Battles have been fought in the USA over exactly what should appear in textbooks and whether certain scientific ideas should be allowed in the classroom, depending on the persuasions of the groups running any particular school.[4] There is a real sense of anxiety, frustration, and sometimes outright anger as those on either side worry about the possibility of wrong ideas damaging young minds.

Although the religion–science tension is a major headline grabber, it is not the only science-related area in which strong opinions are held. We have identified a large piece of furniture in our darkened room, yes – but it is not the only one.

Science the Saviour

To many people, science offers hope. As those clever scientists in white coats work away in the lab, they discover new facts and new techniques which will bring us closer, every day, to a perfect world. The major victories of science in the past remind us that great things can be achieved, and it becomes possible for some to believe that all of our problems will eventually be eliminated by the power of the scientific method. It is a hope that lies behind these words from Pandit Nehru, the first prime minister of India:

> It is science alone that can solve the problems of hunger and poverty, of insanitation and illiteracy, of superstition and deadening custom and tradition, of vast resources running to waste, of a rich country inhabited by starving people.[5]

Here, science itself is the hero. It is easier to hold this view as a non-scientist, since the pressure is firmly placed on the shoulders of those in the profession, but many scientists see things this way too. Royal DSM, a life-sciences company based in the Netherlands has a website entitled "Science can Change the World". It reminds visitors of successes against smallpox, acid rain, and the hole in the ozone layer. This triumphant message champions their staff:

> A handful of inspirational people – that you've probably never heard of – are proving that science doesn't just change the game. It can change our world.[6]

Is this optimism and positivity justified? Is it true that science is the process by which people with big ideas and big brains save the world? Would it be more realistic to say that this is a rather rose-tinted picture, or even a way of handing over responsibility to anonymous laboratory superstars? Whatever the answers to these questions, there is at least one other reason that our governments have put forward for doing science – saving the world, it seems, is not always enough.

Science the Moneymaker

Money talks – and we could hardly expect science to carry on without listening. With eighteen of the top one hundred companies in Britain being directly involved in the sciences[7] (and many others indirectly

LET THERE BE SCIENCE

linked), there is clearly cash to be made if you can get your experiments to work well. These organizations spend almost unimaginable amounts on squeezing a few more decimal points of efficiency out of their devices, or on updating them with an all-new version.

Take, for example, the average cost of bringing a single new pharmaceutical drug to market: *Scientific American* magazine calculated it to be a staggering £1,700 million in 2014.[8] This many pound coins stacked as a tower would be as tall as 600 Mount Everests; laid out in a line, they would almost completely encircle the Earth. Alternatively, and undoubtedly more usefully, every single person in the world could be given 23 pence.

These extraordinary numbers are not lost on leaders around the world. They know very well that science and money go together. Here is why the UK government thinks it should fund scientific research:

> The mission of each research council has been changed to meet the needs of users and to support wealth creation... thereby enhancing the United Kingdom's competitiveness and quality of life.[9]

This is almost unexpectedly honest. There is no mention of saving the world, unless perhaps that is what is meant by improving quality of life. It could be argued that "meeting the needs of users" could be about winning victories over suffering, but there is no denying the strong economic nature of the statement. The government will put money into science, yes – because it believes it will get even more money back out.

Interestingly, this line of argument is not only found in parliamentary papers: it is also used to persuade young people to study science. The top five subjects for graduate salaries in the UK are all sciences, as are nine of the top ten. The Institute of Fiscal Studies ran a presentation in 2013 with the rather clunky title *Why you should study maths (and science and computing) at A-level*. After working through over thirty slides of monetary calculations, they concluded: "it is very likely to earn you more money!"[10]

Science the Spoiler

Most people would not know the name Val Valentino, but a significant number have seen him at work. He is the Masked Magician who decided to expose the workings of numerous magic tricks commonly performed by other illusionists. His TV show, *Breaking the Magician's Code: Magic's Biggest Secrets Finally Revealed*,[11] followed a fixed format – the Masked Magician would perform the illusion as it was originally intended and then (after a commercial break, of course) would do it again, this time showing the method.

Watching this programme could bring forth a variety of emotions: excitement and bewilderment at first, speculation and curiosity before the reveal, satisfaction and closure when enlightened. Not everyone, however, felt fulfilled. In fact, many didn't. The final revelation, which seemed to promise so much, often led to disappointment.

The teleporting girl, it turned out, was actually an identical twin. The coin entered the bottle through a secret hole in the bottom. There was a trapdoor under the casket. The levitation used strong, thin wires. The problem with all of this was the loss of a sense of wonder. It is more fun for many, it would appear, *not* to know what is going on. Commenting on a YouTube video of the show, a user called *cromthor* writes:

> In spite of what we all feel (we WANT to know the secret), our pleasure as spectators is to be fooled, to see something that's IMPOSSIBLE! We want to know the secret, but once we do, let's face it: we're disappointed and our pleasure is gone.[12]

Interestingly, some eminent figures from history describe science in almost the same way. John Keats, the great Romantic poet, would probably empathize with *cromthor's* comment. We see the same type of complaint in one of his poems, "Lamia", from 1820:

> Do not all charms fly
> At the mere touch of cold philosophy?
> There was an awful rainbow once in heaven:
> We know her woof, her texture; she is given
> In the dull catalogue of common things.
> Philosophy will clip an angel's wings,
> Conquer all mysteries by rule and line,
> Empty the haunted air, and gnomed mine
> Unweave a rainbow.

Keats's protest is that science is acting like the Masked Magician. It takes elements of the world which inspire wonder and, in explaining them, strips away their magic. As far as Keats is concerned, science ruins things that were once beautifully mysterious, mutating them into nothing more than boring scientific laws or information. Science, he says, unweaves rainbows.

Science the Monster-Maker

Another Romantic icon – Mary Shelley's *Frankenstein* – is proving to have a far deeper influence within modern, cutting-edge science than might have been expected from a novel written in the 1830s. A cautionary tale, in which a monster is created by Dr Frankenstein using "science", it has been hijacked by mainstream media. They use it to express concerns about the damage scientists might possibly be doing as they meddle with natural processes.

Ignoring the actual point of the book (it is only when the monster is unloved and dismissed that he becomes a threat), the story has now become that science is often unnatural and will lead to disaster of some sort. Playing on this fear, it is now standard journalistic style to add "Franken" to the start of different words, forming a new "science-is-bad" vocabulary. Frankenfoods (those that are genetically modified) are the most common example, but other applications include Franken-tadpoles (with eyes on their tails) and Franken-water (recycled from human waste).[13]

This is a deep-seated narrative in our culture. We worry that "messing with nature" will cost us heavily in the long run. A newly published book by Jean-Pierre Fillard asks whether we might be happily bringing about our own end as a recognizable species – it has the terrifying title *Is Man to Survive Science?*[14]

The hugely successful novel-turned-film *Jurassic Park*[15] grabbed hold of a similar idea and ran with it. The Park's team of technicians use "science" to bring living and breathing dinosaurs into the twentieth century. In a key scene, the man funding all of this research is sternly warned by one of the wisely sceptical heroes: "Your scientists were so preoccupied with whether they could that they didn't stop to think whether they should."[16] As the plot develops, his fear is shown to be valid. Science, we learn, makes monsters.

Science the Odd Family Member

It almost seems a rule that, at every extended family gathering, there is one person present who is not quite operating on the same social level as the rest. He or she is welcome, yes, and even enjoyed – but as some sort of curiosity, almost like an exhibit. The quirky enthusiasm and utterly confusing stories are entertaining for a short while, but are really only tolerated because these gatherings don't happen so often.

This is often the treatment reserved for science and scientists in the media. Take, for example, a recent edition of BBC Radio 4's *Today*.[17] It is not unusual for this programme to deal with very complex and subtle ideas related to the arts, the humanities, or politics, and this one was no exception: it discussed, in depth, the philosophy of a French novelist.

By contrast, when scientists were asked to speak about exploding galaxies on the same programme, they were told off for using "difficult language". The term that caused offence – "a simplifying assumption" – was far more straightforward than many of the earlier philosophical phrases.

Similarly, BBC Radio 5 Live's *Seven Day Saturday*, a quick-fire comedy show covering economics, politics, sociology, and more contains a section introduced with the following jingle: "Here comes the science bit – concentrate!"[18] This is more than just a claim that science is difficult, it seems. The implicit suggestion is that science is somehow *different* to other difficult ideas. Perhaps this explains why science and scientists are often treated as a bit of light relief when they turn up in a studio. They are wheeled in to pronounce some fact or another, and the following interactions with the hosts are usually either awkward or comical. The message is clear: science is not "normal".

Science the Spooker

People can occasionally be hit by a profound revelation: there is an awful lot out there in the world about which they know precisely *nothing*. Questions might range from "how do clouds stay in the sky?" to "who or what am I?" Stopping to think like this can be scary – the questions can get big quite quickly. "What kind of universe do we live in?" "Is there a 'big picture', or not?"

Science is unafraid to tackle questions like these, and it can be tempting to just let scientists get on with it – but, on occasion, there remains the nagging sense that that is not going to be enough. Take the experience of author Bill Bryson, for instance:

> I was on a long flight across the Pacific, staring idly out the
> window at moonlit ocean, when it occurred to me with a certain

uncomfortable forcefulness that I didn't know the first thing
about the only planet I was ever going to live on.[19]

Not prepared to let this thought go, Bryson decided to do something
about it, which resulted in the wonderful book *A Short History of
Nearly Everything*. Yet, for every new book spawned, there will be
thousands of people who stay quietly spooked as it dawns on them
that they don't know the answers to some questions that might just
be very important.

George Steiner, the hugely influential thinker, has also been
unsettled by the mysteries of the material world around us. He,
however, came to the conclusion that scientific study cannot then
"unspook" us. Resolution, he says, must be found elsewhere:

> Only art can go some way towards making accessible, towards
> waking into some measure of communicability, the sheer
> inhuman otherness of matter...[20]

Steiner is deeply bothered by the "inhuman otherness" of the
universe, but has given up on science as the tool to deal with it.
Thinking about science, he implies, can certainly get us spooked –
but *only art* provides any meaningful answers.

Plotting Our Course

Let us review our findings. What have we seen, now that the light is
on? The what-is-science-and-what-is-it-for room has indeed proved
to be a cluttered one. Even a quick glance around has revealed several
large items that need to be taken into account. To some, science is
the enlightened arch-enemy of faith, or the saviour of the world, or a
money-spinner. To others it is a rainbow-unweaver, a monster-maker,
a quirky uncle, or a quietly haunting spectre.

Our claim in this book – that doing science is a fundamental part of
what it means to be human, and that it works best when understood
as a gift from God – will have to speak to each of these different
views. We need, therefore, to pick out a route that allows it to do so,
hopefully without striking our bonier body parts on something hard
or sharp.

For this reason, we shall take the approach, throughout, of using
stories. Stories get us thinking about *people* – their motivations, hopes,
or pain; their moments of inspiration or moments of disaster. Stories

are how we best understand ourselves and our beliefs. Stories, as we shall see, can be key in the search for a bigger picture.

In Chapter 2, then, we will consider the history of science. When did science really begin? Was it with the computer? With electric circuits? With gravitational theory? Or, perhaps, might science be much, much older than any of these?

In Chapter 3, we will look at the remarkable fact that human beings can even do science at all, and in Chapter 4 we will investigate the process of scientific revolution – how, in reality, does one theory totally overhaul another? Chapter 5 will address the very real (but often hidden) fact that science does not always go smoothly and is often the cause of great pain – and that, despite this, scientific hope persists.

Chapter 6 deals with the still-developing understanding that, in our world, order consistently emerges from apparent chaos, even at the very deepest levels of our current knowledge. Time and again, we find that the uncertainties in this world also make it a suitable home for us – could this point us to a further, more profound truth?

In Chapter 7 we study the importance in science of asking the right questions and then, in Chapter 8, the even greater importance of *love*.

In each of these chapters, our science stories will intermingle with faith stories – the two are bound together far more tightly than some modern commentators might have us believe. The big pictures painted by the history, the people and the findings of science look very much like those that emerge from the pages of the Bible – and we will go on to find, in Chapters 9 and 10, that this connection might just be of universal significance.

So, we have turned the light on and looked around the room. We have planned our course. It is time, now, to step out and start our journey. What *is* science? What is it *for*? And what, perhaps most significantly of all, does all this have to do with *faith*?

2

AN ANCIENT STORY

Science is a way of thinking much more than it is a body of knowledge.

Carl Sagan

Is there anything of which one can say, "Look! This is something new"? It was here already, long ago; it was here before our time.

Koheleth, in Ecclesiastes

So far we have mostly been listening, without much comment, to what different types of people think of science. To some it is a saviour, while others see it as a complete stranger – or even a worry. We have also identified the path we will take in this book: one which allow us to explore the idea that science is a human activity which thrives in the environment of faith. Our first step on this journey is to ask the question "How *old* is science"?

Before we do so, however, we should discuss why this question is at all relevant. What has the history of science got to do with how things look, right now, in a twenty-first century laboratory? What can we learn from its backstory? Why does it matter how old science is?

The issue is this: science is often presented as something that is relatively *recent*, sometimes even just 300 years young. This version of history would suggest that science does not have any long human tradition and is not, therefore, innate or natural to us at all – which would support the "science is a stranger" idea. On top of this, it could pose a serious problem for our ideas about the centrality of faith in true science.

If science really is this new, it would be very hard to make the case that Christianity is integral to it, because Christianity is very old indeed. It has its origins in Old Testament Judaism, and its central figure – Jesus Christ – walked the earth two millennia ago. If science arises naturally from this ancient faith, as will be proposed, we should expect to find science stories appearing equally early – not just in the last few centuries.

We can put this the other way around: if science only makes an appearance fairly late in the day, it is far more likely to be a secular construct and far less likely to be related to Christian thinking. It is important, then, to know just how far back in time we can go and still find something recognizable as science – for this will either support or weaken our claim that science flows from faith.

The idea that science is young is mainly due to two slightly vague "stories" about its supposed past. These two stories are rarely told as a whole, as they will be below; instead, bits and pieces of them float around out there in the ether – allowing grand, overarching ideas to build up in our minds. These fragments can be found inhabiting Internet forums, classrooms, media interviews, and even the occasional book or video, each doing their little bit to contribute. When these are all combined, we end up with the following:

Story One – In the past, philosophers (especially Greek ones) believed that the universe was made up of both the physical and the spiritual. The physical was imperfect: spoiled and dirty somehow. The spiritual, on the other hand, was pure and wholesome. In some versions of the story, the physical was thought of as a "damaged" version of the spiritual. When pursuing truth, therefore, it was considered far more important to think about the spiritual "ideals" than it was to investigate anything more "earthy".

For this reason, philosophers (such as Aristotle) would not actually carry out experiments, but would instead discuss ideas. As an example, if someone wanted to know how a ball might move through the air when thrown, the last thing he or she would do was actually throw a ball. The preferable course of action was to sit down and talk through different theories until the most elegant or beautiful "truth" was agreed upon.

This way of thinking was held to so strongly that it was only much, much later, when brave new scientists (such as Galileo in the seventeenth century) were prepared to do experiments, that we really learned anything.

A Google search of "Galileo vs Aristotle", for instance, opens up a whole world of variations on this story. For now, though, let us move on to our second science-is-new narrative.

Story Two – In the past, the reason that people were "religious" was that they did not know very much. They only had God or gods to explain the things that they observed, so they made up mystical stories and, over time, these solidified into rigid spiritual doctrines with little or no evidence to support them.

Nowadays, though, we use science to explain those same things. The scientific method has overpowered the old religion and superstition, finally leading us to the truth. This process – so the story goes – of brave new scientists freeing us from the shackles of fairy-tale faith began in earnest in the seventeenth and eighteenth centuries, a period known as the Enlightenment or the Age of Reason. It has continued since then, and victory after victory has been won over the naive mysticism that held humanity back for so long.

Are either of these stories accurate? Both claim that real science is a relative newcomer. Both claim that real science had to wait for centuries before it could eventually push philosophy and/or religion out of the way. Is this right, or wrong, or simply misleading?

Well, there is certainly much to be said in favour of Story One. In *The Republic*, the ancient Greek philosopher Plato (428–348 BC) describes some prisoners chained to the wall of a cave, a state they have been in from birth. On this wall they can see moving shadows – cast by a fire – of the people and objects outside the cave. This is the only information they have to determine what they can about the wider world.

Should one of them be freed, however, he or she would now be able to explore this greater reality fully – and Plato then argues that a good philosopher does just that. The shadows, he says, represent the physical world we live in; the objects casting them stand for a deeper, spiritual realm.

Story One claims that this theory permeated Western thought, thereby promoting philosophy and inhibiting hands-on science. Alfred North Whitehead (1861–1947), the mathematician, scientist, and philosopher, agrees: "The safest general characterisation of the European philosophical tradition is that it consists of a series of footnotes to Plato."[1]

There is further support available for Story One. It is true, for instance, that Galileo helped to popularize the use of real, physical experiments when determining scientific laws. This can be seen from his 1638 work, *Two New Sciences*, which contains a fictional exchange between three characters.[2] These are *Simplicio*, who follows the old ways of Aristotle, and *Salviati* and *Sagredi*, who speak (here) for

Galileo. On the topic of whether two balls of different mass would fall at different speeds, *Salviati* says:

> I greatly doubt that Aristotle ever tested by experiment whether it be true.

Simplicio wants to defend Aristotle, but his argument is rather weak:

> His language would seem to indicate that he had tried the experiment, because he says: "We see the heavier"; now the word see shows he had made the experiment.

Sagredi, however, then applies the killer blow:

> But I, Simplicio, who have made the test, can assure you that a cannon ball weighing one or two hundred pounds, or even more, will not reach the ground by as much as a span ahead of a musket ball weighing only half a pound.

Galileo is saying that scientific experiment beats idealistic philosophy because it is prepared to get its hands dirty. If you want to know the truth, he claims, you have to try things out in practice. Story One would have us believe that this is how science slowly started to get going. Before this, philosophical concepts were more important than actual evidence. Real science, therefore, began a few hundred years ago – science is "new". Can Story Two reinforce this finding?

Once again, we can quickly find some evidence for its central assertion: that religion squashed science until the seventeenth-century Enlightenment. After all, Martin Luther (1483–1546), one of the spiritual leaders of the Christian Reformation, has some astonishingly strong negative views on "reason":

> [Luther] called reason the "devil's bride," a "beautiful whore," and "God's worst enemy" and said: "There is on earth among all dangers no more dangerous thing than a richly endowed and adroit reason." Again: "Reason must be deluded, blinded, and destroyed" and "faith must trample under foot all reason, sense and understanding".[3]

We can contrast this with a quote from David Hume (1711–76), one of the key figures of the Age of Reason. He champions reason, saying that only rational thought and evidence will do:

> If we take in our hand any volume; of divinity or school metaphysics, for instance; let us ask, Does it contain any abstract reasoning concerning quantity or number? No. Does it contain any experimental reasoning, concerning matter of fact and existence? No. Commit it then to the flames: for it can contain nothing but sophistry and illusion.[4]

Even from these quotes alone, we can feel the weight of Story Two. In the first, we hear a religious leader utterly dismiss any idea of free thought, study, or logical analysis. In the second, we hear a courageous critic of religion taking a stand, declaring boldly that only statements which have been subjected to scientific testing should hold any authority. It really does sound like science is at war with religious belief – that it is fighting to tear itself free.

Putting these two stories together, then, seems to paint a rather straightforward picture – that science is a relatively new thing. Kept at bay for most of human history by groundless philosophy and religion, it has only made an appearance fairly recently. The overall argument is a clear one: "science" arrived a few centuries ago; "science" has made fantastic, faultless progress since then; science will – one day – win out completely.

We should be wary, though, of drawing any final conclusions without a more careful look. As the biblical book of Proverbs advises us: "The one who states his case first seems right, until the other comes and examines him."[5]

Is science really only a recent development? Can science only flower once faith is vanquished? To answer these questions, we will first need a definition of "science" to work with. Once we have one, we shall look at some modern scientific work to make sure our definition is reasonable. From there, we will begin to go backwards in time, searching for older and older science stories. How far back can we get?

Science: A Definition

Where can we find a workable definition of science? Thankfully, we are not the first to ask that question, and there are some key ideas that are widely agreed upon already – the Wikipedia entry for "scientific method" provides a helpful synopsis, for example.

The general consensus is this: observations should be made; there should be an attempt to explain them; there should be some evidence both of further experiment and of analysis. Some have suggested that mathematics is essential too, but we shall come back to that issue shortly.

The associated term "scientist" does arrive fairly late in history, and is first used in the 1830s. It would be hasty, however, to conclude that there could not have been scientists before the word itself existed. Various characters from history have been put forward as the "first scientist", but the simple fact that there is no one candidate upon which experts agree suggests that the lines cannot be drawn as clearly as some might like.

In his book – which is actually entitled *The First Scientist* – Brian Clegg argues that the honour should go to Roger Bacon, who was born in AD 1214. He gives the following reason, among others: "He would not accept pure argument; everything should be subjected to experiment."[6]

Clegg also uses Bacon's embracing of mathematics as evidence for supporting his case. This already takes us back long before the 300 year age of science in Story One. If we are not careful, however, we could find ourselves ruling out whole periods of history and hundreds of individuals if we make our definition too tight. Any idea that there was neither "science" nor "scientists" before AD 1200 might turn out to be unnecessarily extreme.

Is it possible, then, that we can take a slightly different approach and broaden the definition out a little, without compromising our essence of observation, explanation, and experimentation? The answer to this is a resounding "yes". We can do it by considering an older name for science; a name that some would say is actually a far better one.

The British scientist Isaac Newton (1642–1726) is reckoned by many to be the greatest human mind in history. He made many leaps forward that are still taught in classrooms today. His laws of motion are in the specifications of every high school physics course worldwide, and his work on gravity revolutionized the way people have thought about our universe ever since. Incidentally, Newton rules himself out of the running for "first scientist" status, acknowledging that he had built on the work of others before him. He wrote in a letter to his colleague Robert Hooke (1635–1703) that: "If I have seen further it is by standing on the shoulders of Giants."

The reason for introducing Newton at this early stage of the book – he will be mentioned again – is actually so we can consider a term that is very helpful in understanding what true science might really mean. Newton's mammoth three-book masterpiece, for which he is best known, is given the Latin title *Philosophiae Naturalis Principia Mathematica* or, when translated into English, *Mathematical Principles of Natural Philosophy.*

The reason for this is that "natural philosophy" was used to mean "science" long before the word "science" was coined. In fact, we can go further – "philosophy" is Greek for "the love of wisdom", so the full meaning of natural philosophy is "the love of wisdom about the things in nature".

This is a wonderful way to describe science. "Loving wisdom about nature" is a great picture for us to have in mind when we think about science working to its full human potential. Watching the world at work, thinking about how it might be happening, testing out ideas, and using them for something new is the dream scenario for scientists. The "Eureka!" moments of discovery, when wisdom about nature is won, are what all scientific professionals (and amateurs) hope for. This term – natural philosophy – is perfect for guiding us towards a good definition of science.

Here we go, then: we will count something as true science if – and only if – we can show it meets three distinct criteria. First, there must be observation of something in nature. Second, there must be a discussion of a possible physical cause. Third, there should be some form of analysis or testing involved. This last requirement might be through planned experiment, physical interaction, or by further observation.

We must bear in mind that, just as with music or art or any human activity, what was done many centuries ago might look very different to its descendants today. A twelfth-century painting, for instance, follows many artistic "principles" not used now, but we would never reject it as art. Similarly, the science we find far in the past might also "look" different in some ways, but if it meets our three criteria, it is science nonetheless.

In light of this, we will not treat the use of accompanying mathematics as strictly necessary. It is the attitude, aim, and approach of those involved that we are concerned with – the Carl Sagan quote from the beginning of this chapter captures this well. The science we are looking for is really driven by *"a way of thinking"*.

Science is a curiosity that leads to actually doing something. It is being dissatisfied with not knowing something and chasing down the answers. It is natural philosophy. When people look at the world around them and ask how it works "on the inside" (in a real and practical sense), this is scientific thinking. When they try their ideas out, analyse the results, and draw conclusions, this is scientific practice. Whenever and wherever we can identify these sorts of human behaviour – regardless of historical style, language, or fashion – we can be confident in calling it a love of wisdom about nature. We can be confident in calling it *science*.

Now that we have a definition in place, we can begin our trip back through time, starting with a thoroughly modern example of natural philosophy.

AD 1997 – The Jelly That Shouldn't Have Been There

Most people will (hopefully) be able to remember from their school days the key idea that physical matter is made up of particles. These particles, as the lessons explain, can be arranged in different ways, forming solids, liquids, or gases. There are, however, other possibilities. Many different types of particle arrangements exist, and some of these could be described as being "in between" these famous three – like jellies, the subject of our first study.

It is tempting, initially, to think of a jelly as a solid. However, the edible jellies that we leave to "set" in a fridge should help us realize that this is incorrect. These desserts are made mostly of water, and water is a liquid at fridge temperatures. This means that the jelly – or at least, nearly all of it – is also a liquid. Why, then, does it not flow away? The answer lies in its particles, and in the unusual way that they are arranged.

In a jelly, a few of the particles are joined together in very long, tough strings, called macromolecules. These long strings are criss-crossed over each other in all directions, forming a network. This network holds the overall structure of the jelly in place, with the liquid particles free to move and slide within it.

Provided there are enough macromolecules about, the liquid can be held in any shape – hence jellies shaping to the mould. The tangled networks still allow flexibility, which gives rise to the characteristic "wobble". This is all reasonably well understood: scientists working in the field can actually calculate the number of macromolecules needed to form any given jelly, for instance.

When, therefore, a young graduate student studying in the 1990s managed – accidentally – to turn a liquid into a jelly without adding any macromolecules at all, it caused great surprise and great confusion. Having ruled out the possibility of an error, this new jelly suddenly found itself in need of explanation. The student had indeed added something to the liquid: a set of minuscule objects called *peptides*.

Peptides, however, are molecules only a few atoms long. They are nowhere near the length of the macromolecules; they have no hope whatsoever of "trapping" liquids.

A perplexed – but utterly fascinated – group of chemists called in both physicists and biologists for help. After a while, it was actually an inspired guess that opened up the way to solving the problem. Perhaps, it was suggested, the short peptides were "turning into" long macromolecules via some unknown process. Sure enough, upon further investigation, it was found that the tiny peptides were constantly "jiggling around" in the liquid – more on this jiggling later – and, at times, were actually *sticking* to one another.

Over a long enough period of time, the peptides would glue themselves together into long "tapes". These tapes then tangled up and around each other, mimicking the role of macromolecule strings, and forming the jelly. All this happened without any extra intervention from the scientists. The peptides did it all by themselves; they bounced around and crashed into each other over and over again. Each collision held a small chance of sticking – add these chances up, though, and whole tapes appear.

With the use of high-detail imaging equipment designed to see individual molecules, the resulting structures were ultimately seen "on camera", and a previously unknown physical process had been formally identified. Subsequently, the formation and behaviour of these tapes has been found helpful in understanding Alzheimer's disease, during which similar structures self-assemble and cause damage to the brain.

Can we count this story as science? How does it match up to our definition? Well, there was certainly observation. There was also a suggested cause, based on an initially hidden interior structure. There was testing and there was further analysis. It matches what we said we were looking for, so we can reasonably refer to it as science – a conclusion which will be of great relief to the journal *Nature*, the publisher of the findings.[7]

Before we move on, we can note a few more brief points. First, the outcome of the jelly story was the ownership of more wisdom about nature. Second, this was both a frustrating and joyful episode, which indicates the presence of deep human involvement – even, maybe, of *love*. We have, therefore, seen our first instance of natural philosophy in its truest sense. We shall now jump back more than a century and see if we can find any more.

AD 1828 – The Jiggling That Wouldn't Stop

Robert Brown (1773–1858) has the unfortunate distinction of being best known for a discovery that he never managed to fully understand. His shortfall was not through lack of effort, as we shall see, but more due to the fact that the scientific world was not yet ready to provide an appropriate explanation. Brown died in 1858; his hugely important observation was eventually made clear in 1905. So what was it?

A hugely talented botanist, Brown mainly concerned himself with the science of plants. It was he who first noticed that plant cells contained a nucleus, providing a key moment in biology. As significant as this observation was, many would say that it is surpassed by one of his others, a story that began when he spotted something odd about pollen grains.

Brown wanted to study the behaviour and structure of these little objects up close, so he put them in water and watched them intently as they hung there, suspended in the clear liquid. As he examined them, he spied some even smaller particles, ejected from the grains. These tiny specks were doing something strange: they jiggled around, with no discernible pattern. Waiting for them to settle down, Brown found, was pointless; the jiggling never stopped. Extraordinary as it might be, these miniature particles appeared *alive* – had the naturalist managed to find the building blocks of life itself?

It did not take long for Brown to decide that he hadn't; some simple tests ruled it out. He tried the same experiment with non-living material like chalk dust, and it jiggled around too. Clearly, this unpredictable and unending movement was due to something other than the particles themselves. One by one, he ruled out possible causes: light, magnetism, vibration in the room, convection currents in the water, electricity, and more.

Over time, Brown began to realize that he was not going find an answer. He knew in his heart that this jiggling was incredibly important and suspected – rightly – that it would become a foundation stone for future science. As a result, he did something incredibly selfless: he wrote up all his results and resisted the temptation to give any explanation at all. Displaying extraordinary self-control, Brown kept back his own speculative theories for fear of misleading those who followed him.

Several decades later, Albert Einstein made the breakthrough that Brown couldn't – although he did have several significant advantages over his predecessor. Atomic theory was far better established by now, and the idea that matter (including water) was made up of atoms was widely accepted. Importantly, the accompanying maths predicted that atoms would writhe around in a state of constant, haphazard motion and that they would be invisible – even under a microscope. The wriggling motion, Einstein showed, gives rise to the property of "heat".

Could this always-moving-atoms idea be the key to Brown's mysterious jiggling? Einstein wondered if the hyperactive water atoms might somehow be energetic enough to move particles far larger than themselves – perhaps even chalk dust. Amazingly, his calculations showed that they would be. The chaotic, non-stop motion that Brown had recorded was being caused by chaotic non-stop motion on an even smaller scale – one that could not be seen.

As time has gone on, this ever-present movement of atoms has been proved to be more and more vital. This will be discussed further in Chapter 6, but for now it is worth making the following point: many biological processes are utterly dependent on this tumbling, erratic behaviour. Without it, we would not be here. In that sense, we can offer encouragement to Brown: he had indeed found one of the building blocks of life.

AD 1225 – The Bishop 700 Years Ahead of His Time?

The word "medieval" is often used to describe something that is backward, or cruel, or simply embarrassing. History exalts the intellectual prowess of the ancient Greeks and delights in the thinking of the Enlightenment – everything in between, though, seems rather a waste of time.

Thankfully, this common picture has increasingly been coming under challenge, and Robert Grosseteste, a former Bishop of Lincoln, is one of the reasons. In fact, Grosseteste has also been lauded as a potential "first scientist". Astonishingly, during the first half of the thirteenth century, he managed to write about early forms of both "wave–particle duality" in matter – a key feature of quantum mechanics – and cosmology's "big bang" theory.

The initial idea that matter might be composed of tiny little particles called atoms had existed from at least 400 BC, so there was nothing novel about it by the time that Grosseteste began his scientific career. Despite this, there was a problem that refused to go away – that of solidity.

It is clear that a chair or a book is solid – it takes up space, and it is not (obviously) compressed when a force is applied to it. But why does it behave like this? One simple answer is that atoms themselves are solid. This, however, was hardly satisfactory. It just pushed the problem one stage further: why are atoms solid?

Grosseteste decided to take this problem on, and not just by philosophy: he would apply observation and possibly experiment. The key step in his work *De luce* ("*On light*") was to consider the behaviour of light – and compare that to the behaviour of atoms.

Grosseteste demonstrated that light could "fill up" spaces as part of its normal behaviour. Open a shutter in a dark room, for instance, and the light would "expand" in some sense, filling the room. He saw this as a type of "natural extension" of light. Perhaps something like light was allowing matter made of tiny point-like atoms to do something similar, expanding by a process like this until the mixture of atoms and light took up space and was solid?

This might sound very odd indeed – and it is – but it is not all that far from the truth. Quantum mechanics (more detail in Chapter 4) describes particles as behaving like light; sometimes even spreading out when passing through gaps, very close to the behaviour Grosseteste guessed. Beyond any doubt whatsoever, Grosseteste engaged in science. He observed, he experimented (he writes about using different materials to obtain different colours of light), and he formed theories. It is little wonder, then, that he made another extraordinary leap.

Connecting the expansive behaviour of light with solidity in materials, Grosseteste then suggested that the universe might have begun with an explosion of expanding light, eventually leading to the formation of solid matter. Once again, his instincts were correct. They match up quite remarkably with some of the main ideas of the big bang theory, an idea which now dominates our thinking about both space and time.

This is no unscientific mysticism. Grosseteste opened shutters, sat on chairs, tried things out, and then formulated functional models which would surface once more, centuries later, in "modern" physics. This might not quite be science as we would recognize it, but it is most certainly science *as a way of thinking*.

AD 703 – The Monk, The Philosopher, and the Salt Water Debate

Moving back yet further in time, we find a most interesting character known as the "Venerable Bede" (672–735). Bede was a monk, and is sometimes called the "Father of English History" because of his *Ecclesiastical History of the English Speaking Peoples*. Unbeknown to many, however, Bede also wrote about mathematics and science. We will take a very brief stop on our journey to look at one particular entry from *On the Nature of Things*.

Like solidity, the issue of how the sea could be salty when it was only ever fed by fresh river water also nagged at those who loved wisdom about nature. Pliny the Elder (AD 23–79), a naturalist and author, championed the theory that river water sank when it entered the already salty sea and then returned to the rivers from the bottom of the sea via underground tunnels. Despite Pliny's great reputation, Bede is unafraid of taking him on:

> But fresh waters flow above salt waters, for they are lighter;
> the latter certainly, being of a heavier nature, better sustain the
> waters poured over them.[8]

Here, Bede says the tunnel theory is wrong – because fresh water floats on salt water. He counters the concept with an observation, an explanation, and even an experiment. This is science through and through.

AD 379 – The Dying Sister and the Mind's Eye

Gregory of Nyssa and Basil the Great are two of the three "Cappadocian Fathers", men who were responsible for some major theological decisions made in the early life of the Christian church. This included the writing of the Nicene Creed, the opening lines of which will be familiar to many: "We believe in one God, the Father, the Almighty, maker of heaven and earth…" Gregory and Basil were brothers. They also had an older sister, Macrina, precious to them for her love, her insight, and her wisdom; they even called her "Teacher".

In AD 379 Basil died. Gregory went to visit Macrina to seek comfort, only to find that she was also on her deathbed. To reassure Gregory of the hope of resurrection and the promise of the three being together again, Macrina seeks to prove to Gregory that the essence of a person – the "mind" – is eternal.

Her intention is to demonstrate that the mind has an existence beyond just the physical processes of the body, and she chooses scientific observation to make this point. The extract we will study now is fairly long (it might take more than one read to absorb fully) but it is worth looking at in its entirety:

> It is by an abuse of language that a jar is said to be "empty"; for when it is empty of any liquid it is none the less, even in this state, full, in the eyes of the experienced. A proof of this is that a jar when put into a pool of water is not immediately filled, but at first floats on the surface, because the air it contains helps to buoy up its rounded sides; till at last the hand of the drawer of the water forces it down to the bottom, and, when there, it takes in water by its neck; during which process it is shown not to have been empty even before the water came; for there is the spectacle of a sort of combat going on in the neck between the two elements, the water being forced by its weight into the interior, and therefore streaming in; the imprisoned air on the other hand being straitened for room by the gush of the water along the neck, and so rushing in the contrary direction; thus the water is checked by the strong current of air, and gurgles and bubbles against it.[9]

Let us attempt to pick out the key points. Macrina is describing a jar which one might at first describe as *empty*, but is actually *full* of air. This can be shown by first letting the jar sit on the water and float, then by pushing it downwards so that its neck is below the surface.

If the jar was empty initially, water could just immediately fill it up, but Macrina points out that this doesn't happen – the air must leave the jar if water is to enter it. This leaving and entering occur simultaneously, resulting in *bubbles* and *gurgles* as the upwards-moving air and downwards-moving water fight it out.

Macrina's aim here is to show that the mind is able to think things through at a level beyond basic observation. If we were purely physical entities, she argues, we would be limited to physical deductions: we would not be able to understand the jar as being full of air, because we cannot see it.

The mind, however, *can* "see" it – by using reasoning. Macrina reinforces this fact by referencing the phases of the Moon. Although the eye observes the Moon getting bigger and smaller, the mind overrules it – we can "see" a sphere being lit from different angles. That the mind has this ability to go beyond the physical senses, Macrina says, means it is of more than just physical composition. Because of this, there can be hope that the mind will live on, even if the body does not.

Regardless of what we think about this argument or its conclusions, the water jar description is clearly *science*. We have observation, theory, experiment, and even the notion of "seeing" with the mind what the eye cannot – all in the fourth century AD.

A final observation remains before we move on: Gregory writes all this after Macrina's death, which came very soon after this discussion. He confirms later on that he was greatly comforted by her words. Here, then, we see science playing a healing role in the real world of hurt and struggle.

This is a theme which we will find ourselves revisiting many times in this book. Is it possible that science – in the connecting, contemplating way we have defined it – might be able to touch people in ways that they had not perhaps considered before? Can it *heal*? Leaving this thought for now, though, we shall continue our journey back through time.

AD 30 – The Digestive System and Morality

During his three-year teaching ministry, Jesus of Nazareth spoke every bit as much to ordinary townspeople as he did to committed followers or influential thinkers. A gifted and charismatic teacher, he often used analogies from everyday life to make a point. This is particularly helpful to us if we are interested in knowing about life and thought at the time – and, perhaps surprisingly to some, that includes scientific thought.

In the passage below, Jesus – surrounded by onlookers – is addressing accusations that his disciples have broken laws about eating and are therefore "unclean":

> "Listen to me, everyone, and understand this. Nothing outside
> a person can defile them by going into them. Rather, it is what
> comes out of a person that defiles them." After he had left the
> crowd and entered the house, his disciples asked him about
> this parable. "Are you so dull?" he asked. "Don't you see that
> nothing that enters a person from the outside can defile them?
> For it doesn't go into their heart but into their stomach, and
> then out of the body." (In saying this, Jesus declared all foods
> clean.)[10]

After this, Jesus goes on to explain that *what comes out of a person* – qualities such as greed or arrogance – are far more important to God than what they eat. This is clearly a theological teaching, so what is it doing in a science book?

Of note to us here is that Jesus uses a scientific argument to support his message: he talks about the biological functions of the organs. Jesus differentiates between the role of someone's digestive system – their *stomach* – and the moral quality of their overall being. What someone eats, he says, is independent of their goodness. He even implies that this is testable, although the test would not necessarily be a pleasant one.

He does, however, also reference the *heart*, so should we chalk that up as an error? No – the association of the heart with our actions or emotions is not meant here as an anatomical one. It is, rather, a bit like when we talk about being heartbroken or about feeling things in our "gut" or our "bones". The stomach claim is scientific in nature; the heart claim isn't.

Of particular interest to us is this: Jesus makes a clear reference to a known biological fact and uses it to reinforce a spiritual point. He binds science and faith together. One does not squash or hinder the other. This is the type of interaction that has proved so fruitful in the past, as we will come to see. This working together might be seen more often if the core message of this book were to be embraced. Here we have an example of how to use good science to improve our understanding of ourselves – and of our interaction with nature.

Helpful references to scientific ideas and principles pop up elsewhere in the Bible's New Testament, and we will consider more of these in future chapters. Now, though, we will move on to its "prequel", the Old Testament. Since we have, perhaps, become better at spotting science in places that it could previously have been missed, can we find more?

600 BC – Ancient Detox

The Babylonian Empire of Nebuchadnezzar II enjoyed significant development in agriculture, economics, and art. It emerged out of civil war in the region that now encompasses countries such as Iraq, Kuwait, and Syria. As it consolidated, vast quantities of learning were first gathered and then acted on in new, highly effective ways.

Not all the power of the Empire was creative, however. The unfortunate Jews were among many people groups brutally conquered by the Babylonian armies, and the Jewish Temple was ransacked. The bravest and best of their young men were carried off to Babylon, where they were put into the service of Nebuchadnezzar. In the Old Testament book of Daniel, we find the story of four Jews who were hand-picked for the king in this way.

According to the biblical account, Daniel, Hananiah, Mishael, and Azariah were selected by the king's courtiers because they were "handsome, showed aptitude for every kind of learning, were well informed, and quick to understand". During their training in the language, literature, and wisdom of the Empire they were treated very well indeed, with no expense spared. Lavish banquets were provided, with exotic food and drink being imported from all over the Babylonian territories. These feasts, however, presented a major problem to Daniel and his friends.

Being Jews, their diets were tightly regulated by the law of Moses – a law which they believed had been written in person by God – and much of the food on offer in Babylon was banned. The result was a dilemma for Daniel: should he refuse the king's hospitality and, in so doing, risk his very life?

In what would prove to be an inspired decision, Daniel actually proposed a scientific investigation to resolve the issue: a formalized study of the effects of different diets. In his excellent book, *Bad Science*,[11] Ben Goldacre describes this event as the "first clinical trial". The Bible tells us that Daniel said:

> Please test your servants for ten days: Give us nothing but vegetables to eat and water to drink. Then compare our appearance with that of the young men who eat the royal food, and treat your servants in accordance with what you see.[12]

The king's servant agrees to this. At the end of the experiment, he notes that the four men "looked healthier and better nourished". As a result, the diet for all of the participants in the training programme is changed, whether they are Jews or not.

Not only is this clearly science, it is strikingly modern. Many current food-related schemes take this exact approach in their advertising. Many of today's diets or products urge comparison against the alternatives. Daniel – an Old Testament character – intertwined recognizably well-founded scientific methodology with his faith. And, as we shall now discover, he is not alone.

1150 BC – God the Laboratory Technician

Long before the Babylonians successfully conquered the Jews, plenty of other groups had given it a pretty good go. The Midianites and Amalekites were two who had cracks at it, employing nasty strategies such as the systematic destruction of any newly planted crops. As the beleaguered Jewish nation reached desperation point, a young Israelite had a visit from God himself, telling him to take up arms and fight off these oppressors. This man – Gideon – had his doubts. Was this "messenger" really God? Was his message to be trusted? Donning his white lab coat (metaphorically), Gideon devised an experiment to find out:

> "If you are truly going to use me to rescue Israel as you promised, prove it to me in this way. I will put a wool fleece on the threshing floor tonight. If the fleece is wet with dew in the morning but the ground is dry, then I will know that you are going to help me rescue Israel as you promised." And that is just what happened. When Gideon got up early the next morning, he squeezed the fleece and wrung out a whole bowlful of water.[13]

Not content with this result, Gideon designed a follow-up:

> "Let me use the fleece for one more test. This time let the fleece remain dry while the ground around it is wet with dew." So that night God did as Gideon asked. The fleece was dry in the morning, but the ground was covered with dew.

Isn't this just a typical myth from early humanity about an imaginary God and preposterous miracles? Isn't it as far removed from scientific rigour and modern insight as it is possible to be? The existence of God, miracles, or even Gideon himself, however, is entirely beside the point – all we are asking (for now) is this: is it science?

It would appear so, for Gideon begins the process with a hypothesis. If God is *not* interacting with me, he thinks, the fleece and ground will behave the same way: both will be wet or both will be dry. Why? Because that is what normally happens. Scientists call this the "null hypothesis" – the outcome you would expect if there was no "extra" effect present. Gideon's null hypothesis is based on his own observations of the world – of the ordinary behaviour of dew.

After the experiment Gideon analyses the results, finding that there is far more water in the fleece than the null hypothesis predicted.

Like all good scientists should, Gideon then runs a repeat. This time, he allows for the possibility that some unknown but entirely natural process might have made the fleece wet, so he reverses his demand. By doing this, Gideon is ruling out other factors from influencing his results, something all professionals seek to do in the laboratory. Once again, his (new and improved) criteria are met by God. Conceding that the most likely explanation for all this is a divine rather than purely naturalistic one, he forms a conclusion and acts accordingly: "So Gideon and his army got up early and went."

Let us repeat the important point that readers do not need to believe this story (although many, including scientists, do) to see science in it. The Gideon account meets the standards of our definition – in fact, with its null hypothesis, its repeats, and its refinements, it could even be argued to go somewhat beyond them.

Some Bonus Extras

The Old Testament talks scientifically in other places. Sometimes this is in the creation accounts of Psalms, sometimes in the descriptions of metallurgy or of construction, and sometimes in the agricultural pictures given by the Prophets. An example of the latter can be found in Isaiah:

> Caraway is not threshed with a sledge,
> nor is a cartwheel rolled over cumin;
> Caraway is beaten out with a rod,
> and cumin with a stick.
> Grain must be ground to make bread;
> so one does not go on threshing it for ever.[14]

At first, the connection with science is not obvious, but we must remember that agricultural knowledge like this is accumulated through observation, theory, and experiment. Any objection that the process is really only simple trial-and-error can be met with an important counter-argument: much of modern science is trial-and-error, as we shall see. Isaiah's words also remind us that there is a productive relationship to be had between humanity and nature – one that has to be worked at, but can yield much good when pursued properly.

Our last stop on our time-travel adventure is one the oldest books of the Bible – Job. An ancient and poetic story, it centres on Job – a man who unwittingly becomes the subject of a divine test. Beginning the text as a rich, blessed, and successful figure, Job is known as a committed servant of God.

A character called "the Accuser" then appears and makes the claim that Job's commitment is due entirely to his high standing, riches, and quality of life. Disputing this, God allows Job's wealth, family, and health to be torn away, leaving him emotionally distraught and in great physical pain. God is convinced that Job will remain faithful, even in suffering; the Accuser is not.

Totally unaware of this heavenly interaction, Job is mystified as to why his life has fallen apart. His friends who counsel him suspect that he must have done something terrible to offend God, but Job protests his innocence. The poem recounts Job's desperate calls for justice and explanation and his friends' attempts at answers. Only at the end does God himself speak; and Job is eventually restored to an even greater set of circumstances than the one he began with.

Why are we highlighting the book of Job in this way? What is its significance to our thesis? The answer is a relatively simple one: it is packed to the rafters with *science*. We find Job, his friends, and even God addressing scientific topics, sometimes at great length.

Job's complaint to God includes ideas about floods, lightning, and the stars; his friends reference nature repeatedly as they seek – often rather unhelpfully – to "comfort" him. When he finally intervenes, God leads them all on a grand tour of the cosmos – the creation described by the Creator. As we consider our questions about science, we will visit Job again and again.

Science: An Old, Long Story

We began this chapter by considering two stories. Both said that science is "new", and their foundations seemed fairly robust. Real science, they claim, has triumphantly emerged from the ashes of old philosophical and religious beliefs, which have in turn been exposed as shallow and groundless. Evidence is the new standard, and logic the new language.

As we look back through the ages, though, this science-is-new idea doesn't quite hold up. The scientific way of thinking – supposedly so modern – has been there for thousands of years: we find it in the "Jelly Team", in Brown, in Grosseteste, in Bede, in Macrina, in Jesus, in Daniel, in Gideon, and, as we shall see on more than one occasion as we progress, in Job.

Significantly, in each case we have studied, those involved have been people of faith. From one of this book's authors (who worked on the peptide tapes) all the way back to the long-distant Job, the scientific thought we have identified has come from individuals who believe in, and trust, the God of the Bible.

Each one feels no need to separate their faith from their science. In fact, they see them as thoroughly interrelated. Consider the words of Robert Grosseteste, for example, who links wisdom about nature with wisdom about God: "But according to truly wise men, every notice of truth is useful in the explanation and understanding of theology."[15]

Can faith in the Christian God really aid science and benefit the scientist? The Christian faith is one of ancient origins. If science is new, the claim that Christianity encourages its growth would be dealt a heavy blow. Why, we would be able to ask, did this encouragement not make itself obvious much earlier in history? Why did it take so long for science to appear if it supposedly grows out of faith?

We have seen, however, that the story of science is a very old one indeed; it has been there for as long as human beings have been recording their thoughts. Science, as a way of thinking, is most definitely *not* new. It has not arisen from the corpse of faith. Instead, the opposite is true: science has thrived, for millennia, in the presence of belief in the biblical God.

In fact, as we take in this older and grander picture of natural philosophy, it would almost seem that observation, theorizing, and experiment are hardwired into humans. Is this really true? Are we – and the universe around us – somehow *designed* to make science possible? If so, what can we conclude from this? These questions will be the subject of our next chapter.

3

A GIFT AND AN INVITATION

The most incomprehensible thing about the universe is that it is comprehensible.

Albert Einstein

Who has put wisdom in the mind? Or who has given understanding to the heart?

God, in Job

The Trossachs National Park in Scotland manages, somehow, to be both stark and beautiful. Its combination of rugged mountains, wooded walkways, and brooding lochs can prove irresistible to hikers, cyclists, and nature lovers of all varieties. Perhaps the most dedicated of all the souls to visit the region, though, are those who travel with just one goal in mind: to catch a sight of the treasured osprey, or "fish eagle" as it is sometimes called.

Hunted to extinction in the country a century ago, the osprey has been gently reintroduced to the area in more recent years, and with some considerable success. As glorious as it is, however, this majestic bird is far from being the only wildlife highlight on offer in the Trossachs – others which can be seen include lions, elephants, rhinos, and giraffes. Anyone wanting to do so needs simply pay a visit to Blair Drummond Safari Park.

While there, one would be remiss not to take the boat trip around Chimp Island. As the craft glides along, the audio commentary breaks off to warn of the possibility of missiles being thrown at its passengers, and then continues to inform them about the animals they are (hopefully) observing. Listeners are reminded that the chimpanzees share almost 99 per cent of their DNA with people and that they are one of the five great apes "along with bonobos, orangutans, gorillas and, of course, *us*".[1]

One conclusion that could be drawn from this is that the

chimpanzees are *very nearly human*. After all, 99 per cent is pretty much the whole game, isn't it? We are in the same great-ape club, we have the same basic body plans, chimpanzees use tools, and so on. This is all such old news that it can be sounded out over the tour speaker without anyone on board so much as batting an eyelid.

With a little more thought, though, some questions emerge. Does our DNA crossover with any given animal really tell us the "humanness" of it? Is humanness more than just biological information? The fact that human beings were on a man-made diesel boat, touring a man-made island, listening to a man-made broadcast would suggest that, in reality, the gap between the chimps and them might be far more than just 1 per cent. But how so?

Rather than asking what we have in common with other creatures we will, in this chapter, consider what is different about being human. This is by no means an attempt to detract from the wonder of the flora and fauna we share this planet with; we will discover reasons to treasure and care for them later in this book. For now, the question that will occupy us is this: what is it that makes human beings stand out? Three winding threads of human curiosity and ingenuity will lead us into this chapter. The rather unlikely trio of moth larvae, schoolbook geometry, and pomegranates will guide us through some of the key mathematical and scientific revolutions that have shaped our world, leading ultimately to the finest technological achievement of them all.

Like threads on the visible reverse of a half-made tapestry, the picture they make might at first seem rather tangled. At times, we will jump from one part of it to another, leaving some threads loose and hanging as we do. At the end of the journey, though, we should be able to step back and view the whole image clearly.

Once there, we can look again at the biblical account of Job, and at the possibility that it is *God* who made us different – that *he* has placed within us the enquiring and creative spirit that brings so much wonderful scientific success.

You're not Going Out Wearing That!

Sometime in China between 4000 BC and 3500 BC, someone decided to take the cocoon of a moth larva, warm and soften it in water, and unravel it into a single, almost invisible thread. This person (or a successor in the craft) then twisted this thread around itself again and again until the fibre was strong enough to make garments out of. The end product? Silk. This luxurious material is actually the saliva of the larvae – or "silkworms" – and it remained a Chinese secret for nearly 3,000 years.

The technology of weaving on a loom is at least as old as silk and is a simple process if the weaver only wants a plain sheet of fabric. The loom holds a set of slightly separated strands firmly in place in one direction – this is the "warp". The user then threads other strands over and under the first set, alternating as they go – the "weft". Eventually, the whole piece of fabric will hold together.

Plain sheets, though, are just that – plain. If the wearer would like a pattern on their garment, one option is to paint it on with dye. Another is to have the pattern woven in. This second possibility is more intricate and demanding, so it costs more; which naturally makes it more desirable. Throughout history, the world's most rich and powerful people have consistently and loudly demanded beautifully patterned larvae-spit to wear. This was perhaps most true from 1500 to 1750 in Western Europe.

At that time, weaving a pattern into a piece of clothing or a drape required the weaver to switch from the simple over–under–over–under technique to actually planning the image in advance. He or she would then make sure that the correct number of overs was followed by the correct number of unders in sequence across each individual line of the pattern. Slowly the picture would build up – and it was slow, with the most desirable material being processed by master weavers at about one inch a day.[2]

The costs were huge, as were the wages for the best weavers and the demand from the wealthy. Unsurprisingly, anyone who could invent a way to speed up the process stood an excellent chance of making rather a lot of money. We must abandon this particular thread for now, though, and pick it up later, moving instead to a different part of our tapestry.

What's in a Number?

Philosophers of mathematics today are still bitterly embroiled in what seems almost a silly debate: do numbers actually *exist*? There are those who insist that they obviously do; and those equally certain they don't. The answer depends as much on a secondary concern as it does on anything else: how do we know about numbers?

If they exist, they are non-physical; that much is agreed. The problem is that humans don't appear to have any means of detecting the non-physical – sight, smell, and touch are no good. How can we know something exists without discovering it with our senses? If, on the other hand, they don't exist and are just invented within the human mind, then other pieces of the puzzle don't seem to fit. How is it that we all agree that "413" is "413" if "413" has been completely made up? How can we do maths (which is imaginary) that works in the real world (which isn't)?

Can't we just be pragmatic here? We can use maths, after all, so can't we just forget the philosophy and get on with things? This is an acceptable approach, and one that has probably rescued humanity from getting nowhere at all in the sciences, so we shall indeed move on and look at some maths, leaving another thread loose – but we will return to the debate later, when there might be something more useful to add.

The Axiom Nobody Wanted

We have already encountered past heroes credited with being the "Father of" something, and we now find another one: Euclid, the Father of Geometry. Working in Alexandria around 300 BC, Euclid developed a system from which the properties and behaviours of points, lines, and shapes could all be deduced. This system required five starting statements, called "axioms", which had to be assumed to be true; they could not be proved. The first four went, roughly, as follows:

1. It is always possible to draw a straight line between any two points.
2. A straight line will always remain straight no matter how far it is extended.
3. Circles can be any size, and can have any starting point as their centre.
4. All right angles are the same size as each other: 90 degrees.

Each of these seems fairly simple and straightforward – good ground on which to build a complex system of geometry. However, Euclid found that these four statements were not quite enough; one more was needed. His whole system would fall apart unless he also included a fifth foundational claim:

5. Parallel lines never meet.

Like the others, it seems a simple idea, one easy to accept and work with. Appearances, though, can be deceiving; this fifth axiom was to become infamously problematic.

First, there is the issue of phrasing it. The short version above is actually a bit of a cheat, because it uses the word "parallel" without ever stating what it means. Euclid needed to be more thorough than that, but doing so without making things hideously complicated proved to be almost impossible. Here is his final effort, as translated by the historian of mathematics, Thomas Heath:

> If a straight line falling on two straight lines make the interior angles on the same side less than two right angles, the two straight lines, if produced indefinitely, meet on that side on which are the angles less than the two right angles.[3]

Suddenly, the "parallel postulate", as it is sometimes known, seems rather less elegant than when we first met it – but not much can be done, sadly, to simplify it any further than this.

Second, there is the nagging feeling that this convoluted fifth axiom really should not be needed in the first place; could it not be proved, somehow, by using the first four? They are so self-evident, basic, and clear, unlike their cumbersome teammate; surely they should be enough on their own?

Even Euclid, it would appear, did not like the parallel postulate, but he could find no way of putting his geometry together without it. For centuries, amateur and professional geometers alike have tried to show that it could be derived from the first four, but countless triumphant claims of success have always eventually been shown to be false.[4]

Modern mathematics, therefore, is firmly stuck with this pesky axiom. High school students everywhere still study the geometry of Euclid, which is still built on all five statements. Between them, the quintet lead us to the rules we learned growing up; that the angles within triangles add up to 180°, for instance.

The story of this fifth axiom was to become legendary, however. There were astonishing secrets hidden deep within it, the uncovering of which changed science and our understanding of the universe forever. All will be revealed shortly, but first we must read some more from the book of Euclidean geometry, a fresh chapter which welcomes onto the stage a great hero of science and maths: Johannes Kepler.

The Growing Pains of a Sphere

The pomegranate is a fruit which rewards the patient eater. Biting straight into it is a bit of a disaster: much of the mouthful will be of the bitter yellow fibre which holds the (far tastier) seeds in place. Avoiding this foul-tasting material has led to many different methodologies of seed-scoffing; there are even YouTube video guides. Some people use pins to spear the little pink pips and then eat them one at a time. Perhaps it was this slow-paced approach that allowed Kepler the time to observe that the juicy morsels tended to have twelve flat faces – and then to wonder why.

A German astronomer, Kepler (1571–1630) is most famous for carefully working through pages of handwritten data to deduce a formula for calculating planetary orbits. Newton used this formula in his work on gravity, so Kepler is one of Newton's "Giants".

Mulling over the pomegranate problem, Kepler theorized that the seeds would really prefer to be spheres, but that they were being squeezed into this twelve-sided form by each other as they grew. As a result, he believed that the pomegranate was likely to contain the "best" way of fitting the highest number of seeds into the smallest space available:

> [This] packing will be the tightest possible, so that in no other arrangement could more pellets be stuffed into the same container.[5]

Using Euclid's five axioms, Kepler showed that stacking spheres on top of each other so that each one sat in a "gap" formed by others in the layer below – greengrocer style – would lead to twelve "pressure points". These points, in turn, caused the distinctive seed shape that had first drawn his attention.

Kepler's conjecture – that this was the best way of getting spheres close together – was ultimately shown to be correct nearly 400 years later. In 1998, Thomas Hales of the University of Michigan used a computer to solve what had become known as the "sphere packing problem".[6] His program searched exhaustively through every possible arrangement. It turned out that the pomegranate (or Whoever made it) won.

The Computer Looms

Remember all that money waiting to be made by anyone who could improve the speed of weaving silk? Let's introduce the man who hit that jackpot.

Joseph Marie Jacquard (1752–1834) was the son of a master weaver, but showed no real inclination towards either weaving or brilliance in the first half of his life. In the early 1800s though, he produced a machine that would revolutionize silk production, and would form the conceptual basis of the first computers.

His new device, now known as the Jacquard loom, allowed the individual warp threads to be raised or lowered *automatically* so that the weft threads could just shoot through, producing the correct combination of overs and unders for that line of the pattern.

The most significant aspect of his invention was that the loom was instructed to raise or lower threads by use of cards with holes punched in particular locations. These cards were pressed up against needles: if a needle met a hole, it raised its associated thread, and if not, it didn't. This meant that the pattern for that line was contained on the card. By producing these cards in advance, any pattern could be woven by the loom again and again. The end result was that the process of weaving patterns was programmable, repeatable, and twenty-four times faster.

The importance of the Jacquard loom is that it reaches far beyond the textile industry in its influence. Later in the nineteenth century, Charles Babbage – the "Father of the computer" – decided to use Jacquard's information-storing cards in another way. This time, the positions of the holes would tell a series of cogwheels how to rotate; these cogwheels would then produce the results of mathematical calculations which would otherwise have been done by hand. Manual calculations were time-consuming and error-ridden, but engineers and navigators were in great need of them. Babbage's machine, the Analytical Engine, would carry them out mechanically and flawlessly, changing the game entirely.

Sadly, Babbage was thwarted by the sheer cost of the enterprise. His invention required very precise metal-working in its construction, and a lot of it. The whole project became both unworkable and unfundable, and Babbage's complicated handwritten notes on the Analytical Engine also drifted into obscurity until the last quarter of the twentieth century. His Victorian computer promised much, but it was nearly another century before the Information Age truly began, with new technologies far more suitable for programming.[7]

The basic principle of giving initial instructions to a machine and then letting it get on with the heavy lifting remained very much at the heart of computing. From 1900 onwards, various different mechanisms were used in place of the ill-fated cogwheels. Clever mathematical coding meant information could be processed using switches, which were set as either "on" or "off" – just as Jacquard's loom had told each warp thread to be "up" or "down".

The fervent study of electromagnetism (see the next chapter) led to clickety relay switches. The use of electricity for lighting brought forth vacuum tube switches. Both eventually gave way to the development of the semiconducting transistor switches used in computer chips today.

As these information machines became more plausible, however, a problem emerged. When the switches were misread for any reason, calculations could spiral out of hand. Was there any way for the computers to *check themselves* for error? The answer, perhaps amazingly, was yes – and it could be found by revisiting Kepler's pomegranates.

Packjng Sphgres amd Errur Gorrection

This heading is not quite right: each word contains an error. Without errors, it would read "Packing Spheres and Error Correction". Probably most readers were able to autocorrect it in their minds; but what if there had been two, or even three errors in each word? Suddenly the task becomes much harder. This observation was not lost on the early information theorists working with computer communication.

The language that computers speak uses words made of "bits" rather than letters; a bit is either a 1 (switch is on) or a 0 (switch is off). A computer "word" might be 10010 or 110 for instance; a misreading of bits could then deform these into 11010 or 010, leading to incorrect calculations. Was there a way of anticipating and fixing these errors before they occurred? Could a computer be taught to autocorrect a misread bit, in the same way that our brains can autocorrect a mistyped letter?

This was the question that Richard Hamming tackled in his 1950 paper "Error Detecting and Error Correcting Codes".[8] It is a highly technical work, but we will try and capture the essence of it without going into mathematical detail.

Imagine communicating with a friend by phone. The phone line is not a good one, and it is easy to mishear words. One way of ensuring that communication will still work is to agree in advance to only ever use words from a particular list. If any other word is heard, it must be a corruption of the original, caused by noise on the line.

Whenever this happens, the next course of action is simple: check the agreed list and see which word best matches what was heard. That is likely to be what was actually said, and the message can be corrected accordingly. To get this idea to work well, though, it is very important to have a well-picked set of permitted words.

It would be no good having two words on the allowed list which are too similar – RELAY and DELAY for instance. If the word, as received, was "BELAY", it would not be clear which of the two to change it to, since they are almost the same. For this reason, the words on the list must be *different enough* from each other; we could say the words must be "kept apart" somehow.

There are, it turns out, lots and lots of ways of choosing a list of "words" made from 1s and 0s that are different enough. But which list is the best? Words can be made very different quite easily if they are longer, but this means sending more information and requires more processing time. It would be much faster to have short words, but then it becomes very hard to make them different. What Hamming was working on was this: which list of 1-and-0 words gives strong enough error correction (clear differences) in the fastest possible processing time (short words)?

His answer boiled down to the following: the way to keep the words different – to "keep them apart" from each other – was to picture each word as being at the centre of its very own *sphere*. No two word-spheres must be allowed to overlap at all; if they did, those two words were too "close" to each other – too similar. Using this non-overlapping idea would ensure sufficient difference between the words.

As a result, the question "Which list is best?" morphed into "What is the best way of packing word-spheres?" Wonderfully, the answer to this new question had already been found – in Kepler's work on pomegranates. The word list to use fell out naturally from this, and Hamming's error-correcting code was born. As a result, the information revolution has gone from strength to strength.[9]

It is hard to decide which is the more extraordinary fact: first, that error-correcting computers are so closely linked to both the geometry of a fruit and the artistry of silk production, or second, that human beings were somehow able to discover that link. What is undoubtedly true, though, is that together they provide a beautiful example of our insight into the deeply connected structures which can be found in the world of "natural philosophy". We have already seen that this process is not a recent or modern development, but an ancient one; it is even reflected in some of the oldest biblical texts. As we journey onwards, then, perhaps it would be wise to turn to one of them now.

A Gift and an Invitation

In Chapter 2, we introduced the Old Testament character Job – a godly man who had everything stripped from him without being told why. In his quest to find reason and justice behind it all, he thinks deeply about the world around him, often using language that points towards scientific thinking. Let us consider this excerpt, in which Job is meditating on the process of mining:

> Here is a mine for silver
> and a place where gold is refined.
> Iron is taken from the earth,
> and copper is smelted from ore.
> Mortals put an end to the darkness;
> they search out the farthest recesses
> for ore in the blackest darkness.
> Far from human dwellings they cut a shaft,
> in places untouched by human feet;
> far from other people they dangle and sway.
> The earth, from which food comes,
> is transformed below as by fire;
> lapis lazuli comes from its rocks,
> and its dust contains nuggets of gold.
> No bird of prey knows that hidden path,
> no falcon's eye has seen it.
> Proud beasts do not set foot on it,
> and no lion prowls there.
> People assault the flinty rock with their hands
> and lay bare the roots of the mountains.
> They tunnel through the rock;
> their eyes see all its treasures.
> They search the sources of the rivers
> and bring hidden things to light.[10]

This is a passage worth some careful study. Job describes the miners as far more than just ant-like workers; they *search*, they *see*, they *bring hidden things to light.* These adventurers are changing the world around them as they investigate it. Silver, gold, iron, and copper are all worth the effort, as are gems – but not as food, not for mere survival – instead, they are *treasures.* This is a story of curiosity, of a quest, of risks taken to find *nuggets of gold.*

Such intrigue, creativity, and resourcefulness are not shared by the animals mentioned. Human beings are entering territory unknown and unexplored by any other creature. Even the falcon, with its superb eyesight, has not seen what these people are uncovering. The human miners see the hidden structure of the world like no other creature can. This is about breaking new ground, both in reality and in concept. Only humankind can *put an end to the darkness* – both in the mountain and in our understanding.

This message – that we, uniquely, are made to explore, to ask questions, to seek out wisdom, to *bring hidden things to light* – is found again and again in both the Old and New Testaments. The first book of the Bible, Genesis, tells us that we alone are made in the likeness of God himself. We are formed in the image of the Creator of our world. We are given the ability to look around us and *think* about what we see. Consider Paul's words to the church in Rome:

> For ever since the world was created, people have seen the earth
> and sky. Through everything God made, they can clearly see his
> invisible qualities – his eternal power and divine nature.[11]

Not everyone may agree with Paul's conclusions about God, but the claim is certainly clear enough: we are able to study the world, both because that is how the world is made and because that is how we are made.

We can head back to Job to see more clearly how this is so. Near the end of the book, God himself speaks to Job. Instead of providing answers, God asks questions. It is tempting to see this as some sort of divine put-down – as God silencing Job by reminding him of how little he knows compared to his Mighty Creator. Some writers have said just this. Interpreting the catalogue of God's beautiful nature-questions as a wrist-slap does not fit well, though, with what other passages in the book and in the Bible say about God; particularly with what they say about the beauty of an enquiring mind.

An alternative reading, which makes the whole thing hold together with marvellous consistency is this: God is reminding Job of a *Gift* and an *Invitation.* As a human being, Job has been *given* the ability to enquire and reason with genuine hope of success. As

God's image bearer, he has been *invited* to do so, in order to become reconciled with both the wondrous creation around him and the Creator himself.

When God questions Job he is not crushing him. On the contrary, he is calling on him to rise up and act. He calls him to grasp the great privilege and responsibility of having a searching mind, put into him by his Maker:

> Have you journeyed to the springs of the sea
> or walked in the recesses of the deep?
> Have the gates of death been shown to you?
> Have you seen the gates of the deepest darkness?
> Have you comprehended the vast expanses of the earth?
> Tell me, if you know all this.
>
> What is the way to the abode of light?
> And where does darkness reside?
> Can you take them to their places?
> Do you know the paths to their dwellings?
> Surely you know, for you were already born!
> You have lived so many years!
>
> Have you entered the storehouses of the snow
> or seen the storehouses of the hail,
> which I reserve for times of trouble,
> for days of war and battle?
> What is the way to the place where the lightning is dispersed,
> or the place where the east winds are scattered over the earth?
> Who cuts a channel for the torrents of rain,
> and a path for the thunderstorm,
> to water a land where no one lives, an uninhabited desert,
> to satisfy a desolate wasteland and make it sprout with grass?
> Does the rain have a father?
> Who fathers the drops of dew?
> From whose womb comes the ice?
> Who gives birth to the frost from the heavens
> when the waters become hard as stone,
> when the surface of the deep is frozen?[12]

God, wonderfully, is challenging Job to do some *science*. He is telling him that the curiosity and the abilities that allow us to practise science are deep within him – and is pushing him to pursue its call. The Christian worldview gives us the bedrock for carrying out investigations into the world we live in. It tells us that both we, and the world, were made to do it.

The Bible's answer to the mathematical debate we began this journey with is simple but profound: the reason that we can know about numbers, despite their lack of physicality, is because God has *put wisdom in our minds*. Far from being opposed to reason, Christianity gives us the basis for believing two things that are absolutely crucial if good science is ever to be carried out: that we are reasonable beings, and that the world is a reasonable place.

Silk, Spheres, and Space: Divine Assistance?

We have seen in this chapter that some truly extraordinary results have come from human beings studying nature. Moth cocoons and fiddly fruits have not just been ignored or eaten, as they would be by other creatures – even our great-ape clubmates. Instead, the hardwiring of our questioning nature and our innate ability to make scientific progress led from these two seemingly unrelated and innocuous creations to the error-correcting computer that this book is being typed on. The 1 per cent difference in DNA does not tell the story of what it means to be human. Humanness is about creativity, curiosity, capability. It is about *putting an end to the darkness* of ignorance.

There is a loose end remaining here: what of Euclid's troublesome fifth axiom? Well, it turns out that Euclid really had missed a trick after all; as had so many others for so long. He had always limited himself – as had they – to studying points, lines, and shapes as they would behave on a perfectly *flat surface*. Mathematicians in the 1800s, however, began to investigate a revolutionary new idea: shapes drawn onto *curved* surfaces, such as the surface of a sphere.

To their delight, Euclid's first four axioms held, but the fifth one *changed*. In fact, it proved to be different for every differently curved surface. The floodgates opened, and mathematicians played around with every surface they could think of. One of them, Bernhard Riemann (1826–66), created his own entirely new curved geometry from scratch, seemingly just for the sake of it.

Seventy years later, Albert Einstein was putting together his theory of general relativity, which describes the fundamental material of the universe itself (see Chapter 6). Almost unbelievably, he found that the answers to the equations he needed were already there; Riemann had beaten him to it, with the maths that he had "dreamt up". The very substance of space had been unwittingly laid bare by someone studying for study's sake. It would almost appear that humans are *destined* to explain what is around them.

In the light of the stories of larvae, pomegranates, Riemannian geometry, and the Bible passages we have read, it seems that we have a picture emerging. Our argument in this book is that science functions most naturally within a Christian framework. The Bible claims that we have been given a gift in having the ability to understand this world and that we have a divine invitation to do so. It promises that we can have success when we seek to *see all its treasures*.

In the next chapter, we will study how science sometimes needs revolutions to progress, and how the Christian faith offers the best possible grounding for this. For now, however, perhaps we should let the last word in this chapter go to the pomegranate puzzler himself, Johannes Kepler:

> For the theatre of the world is so ordered that there exist in it suitable signs by which human minds, likenesses of God, are not only invited to study the divine works, from which they may evaluate the Founder's goodness, but are also assisted in inquiring more deeply.[13]

4

REVOLUTIONS

You should not be surprised at me saying "You must be born again."

Jesus of Nazareth

It is no exaggeration to say that physics was reborn in the twentieth century.

Paul Davies

In 1975, the British comedy troupe Monty Python released a movie based on the legend of King Arthur. *Monty Python and the Holy Grail*,[1] a surreal farce, featured characters such as "Sir Robin the Not-Quite-So-Brave-As-Sir-Lancelot", the "Killer Rabbit of Caerbannog", and the "Legendary Black Beast of Aaaaarrrrrrrggghhh". Despite the implicit drama of these names, possibly the most famous scene in the production is one which stars a less impressively titled individual: the "Black Knight".

King Arthur comes across this Black Knight while journeying through a forest. The mysterious warrior is in mid-fight and promptly disposes of his opponent in brutal fashion. Arthur is impressed and seeks to recruit this imposing soldier into his army, but the Knight remains ominously silent. Eventually the king gives up and begins to move on – only to be threatened:

BLACK KNIGHT: None shall pass.

KING ARTHUR: I have no quarrel with you, good Sir Knight, but I must cross this bridge.

BLACK KNIGHT: Then you shall die.

A rather one-sided skirmish follows. First, King Arthur cuts one of the Knight's arms off:

KING ARTHUR: Now stand aside, worthy adversary.

BLACK KNIGHT: 'Tis but a scratch.

KING ARTHUR: A scratch?! Your arm's off!

BLACK KNIGHT: No it isn't!

This pattern repeats, with the Black Knight losing his other arm, then his legs. At each setback, he remains utterly in denial, insisting that his injuries are "just a flesh wound" and shouting "I am invincible!" while hopping on one leg. He even continues to yell challenges at Arthur as the scene ends, with the victorious king riding off (on his imaginary horse, naturally).

The problem that the limbless Black Knight has is obvious: his beliefs do not match the emerging facts. He is simply not prepared to change his mind to match his new circumstances. Any evidence before him is dismissed as irrelevant, because he has already decided what the "truth" is. Even having been comprehensively beaten, he still considers himself unbeatable – and, in continuing to hold this view, he is utterly, disastrously *wrong*.

This optimistic stubbornness might be praiseworthy in a soldier, but would we commend scientists for having the same attitude? Would we want our automobile engineers, our cancer researchers, or our food safety officers to stick firmly to their previous convictions if evidence arose to contradict them?

Clearly not. In successful science, observable facts are signposts and should be followed. This is more obviously true in the professions listed directly above, in which the consequences could really be life or death, but the principle should hold even when they aren't.

When there is an obvious clash between observation and theory, the only sensible course of action is to rethink or replace the failing model – even if it is popular or has held sway for a long time. In reality, though, this is not at all easy. Starting all over again often requires far more courage than sticking rigidly to an old, familiar belief.

In this chapter, we will look at one such "start-again story", one in which the emerging and unavoidable facts called into question the current – and very well-established – theory. We will show that, in circumstances like these, the desire for deeper wisdom about reality is so strong that it urges science onwards; even if there is no obvious everyday-world need for it.

Having done this, we shall once again study the Christian faith, in which we will find the foundations of this ability to start again. For it is in the Bible that we discover the origins of the longing for deep wisdom, for the resolution of contradictions, and for following the evidence – wherever it leads.

The Magnetism of Electricity

In the 1780s, Luigi Galvani (1737–98) carried out a series of experiments which led to him stumbling across something bizarre: he could, at times, get a frog's leg to twitch noticeably. This might not seem all that strange, until the detail is added that the leg had already long since been removed from its frog.[2] Building on Galvani's work – and disputing it while doing so – Alessandro Volta (1745–1827) realized that the twitches only happened when two different metals came into contact with the leg at the same time. He used this observation to invent the battery, by alternating and stacking these different metals in a pile of discs – indeed, the French word for battery actually is "pile". For the first time ever, a continuous electric current was available to scientists; this heralded an extraordinary new age of milestones on the road of science.

A brief warning: the speed of our journey through the following series of events may make the reader a little giddy. Science stories, in truth, are far richer and more human than just their bullet-point accounts. In this era, however, so many heavyweight scientists made so many giant leaps forward in such a short amount of time that we simply cannot visit it all in depth.

Nevertheless, it is important for us now to have an overview of this remarkable period of growth as well as the pace at which natural philosophy was able to operate. To describe it as breathless is no exaggeration. With this in mind, let us press on.

Sir Humphry Davy (1778–1829) used Volta's "piles" to perform a process called electrolysis, in which some elements – sodium, for instance – could be separated out from their compounds for the very first time. Effectively, he had discovered them. Others followed his path, with Hans Christian Oersted (1777–1851) isolating aluminium, a hugely significant step for future engineering.

This same Oersted was in the middle of giving a lecture in 1820 when he noticed that the needle of a nearby compass deflected each time he turned his electric circuit on or off. Clearly, electricity was related to magnetism and, whatever the effect was, it was happening from a distance.

Michael Faraday (1791–1867), student and then lab assistant of Davy's, set about investigating this relationship further, and built a working electromagnetic motor. This was a moment of vital importance in science. The new world of electromagnetism had announced itself on the scene with all the force of the Black Knight; and its early victories were to come thick and fast.

In 1823, Faraday liquefied chlorine gas when performing an experiment suggested by Davy, but Davy felt that he was not sufficiently credited in the write-up. As a result, the relationship between the two became strained. The fallout from this was that Faraday moved into other areas of study for a number of years. After Davy's death, however, Faraday returned to electromagnetics and promptly devised a brand new theoretical system: electromagnetic "fields".

Faraday proposed that both electricity and magnetism would spread out, invisibly, into the "empty" space around any magnet or circuit. As they did so, they would affect any other magnets or circuits in that same space. This, he said, would explain the twitching of the compass needle in Oersted's lecture hall.

The notion of these invisible fields was a game-changer. Many top scientists of the day began investigating the idea further. Faraday's work was soon being tied together with the mathematics and observations of famous names such as Charles-Augustin de Coulomb (1736–1806), André-Marie Ampère (1775–1836), and perhaps the greatest mathematician ever to have lived, Carl Friedrich Gauss (1777–1855).

Result after result added to the growing body of work; some came from experiment and some were entirely mathematical. The explosion of understanding that had been unleashed by Volta's batteries was virtually unprecedented. But with so much going on, the new physics was also becoming a rather messy playing field.

The man who finally succeeded in drawing all of this electromagnetic frenzy into a single coherent model was James Clerk Maxwell (1831–79). His extraordinary insights can be reduced down to just four formulae – now known as Maxwell's Equations. Between them, they comprehensively describe the relationship between magnetism and electricity, as well as the exact behaviours of each.

It was a beautiful, breath-taking achievement. All the best findings in the discipline were bound up in these four equations. They were simple and profound, a few strokes of a pen encompassing a whole realm of nature wisdom. The Black Knight of electromagnetism, though still relatively young, was continuing to conquer all before him.

Maxwell's equations showed that Faraday's fields would have waves travelling through them, like ripples across a pond surface. Due to the completeness of his theory, Maxwell was even able to calculate the *speed* of these waves. One can imagine him doing so for the first time: pen or pencil in hand, working through the sums, wondering if there might be a big reveal at the end.

The result was astonishing. These electromagnetic waves, he showed, would travel at 300 million metres per second: *light speed.* Maxwell, incredibly, had "discovered" light itself. Albert Einstein, no stranger to wonderful realizations himself, looks back on Maxwell's breakthrough with something approaching envy:

> Imagine his feelings when the differential equations he had formulated proved to him that electromagnetic fields spread in the form of polarised waves and with the speed of light! To few men in the world has such an experience been vouchsafed.[3]

In the space of less than seventy years, the previously unrelated ideas of electricity, magnetism, and light had been brought together into one beautiful understanding. There existed, everywhere in space, invisible electromagnetic fields. Any disturbances in these fields caused ripples. Those ripples, it was now known, were *light.*

As time went on, this light-wave maths was shown to match well with experiment and all was rosy in the physics garden. Optimism abounded: it seemed that none of nature's remaining secrets would stay uncovered for long. The small areas still hidden would be soon understood; a complete picture of the world was just a few short steps away. The electromagnetic Black Knight appeared invincible, his foes lying defeated around him.

This run of wins, however, was about to come to an abrupt end. Einstein continues his discussion of Maxwell's dramatic calculation with the benefit of hindsight:

> At that thrilling moment, he surely never guessed that the riddling nature of light, apparently so completely solved, would continue to baffle succeeding generations.[4]

But baffle them it did. The Black Knight – against all expectations – was about to start losing his limbs.

Experimental Broadswords

Maxwell's wave theory was both elegant and magnificent. Even now, more than 150 years later, praise is heaped onto the Scotsman. Carl Sagan, the American cosmologist whose definition of science we found so helpful, is one such admirer: "Maxwell's equations have had a greater impact on human history than any ten presidents."[5]

Over the half-decade which followed the publication of Maxwell's model, however, there arose some rather troubling experimental results. In fact, no fewer than three high-profile laboratory investigations struck devastating blows to the electromagnetic-field-and-wave theory of light. We shall analyse each in turn.

Blow Number One: The Problem of Colour

In a surprisingly postmodern fashion, German physicist Heinrich Hertz (1857–94) somehow managed to play the role of wave-theory hero and wave-theory villain simultaneously. In good-guy guise, he demonstrated the existence of Maxwell's waves experimentally by finding radio waves, a type of light that is not visible, but is expected within the model. This provided real-world data that definitively supported the light-ripple hypothesis. As Hertz stated at the time:

> This is just an experiment that proves Maestro Maxwell was right—we just have these mysterious electromagnetic waves that we cannot see with the naked eye. But they are there.[6]

During the same period of work, however, Hertz also laid the groundwork for the theory's undoing. He was the first to observe and report on what would become known as the "photoelectric effect". This curious phenomenon shouted at the physicists that something in their electromagnetic understanding was wrong – and none of them could get it to quieten down. Let us consider why.

At its heart, the photoelectric effect is rather straightforward. First, put some negative electric charge onto a metal; second, shine some light onto it; and third, observe whether or not the charge leaves. It was the not the method, but the results that had everybody stumped: when the charge did escape, it left for all the wrong reasons.

The well-established maths of waves stated that brightness should be the key, with brighter light releasing more charge. Instead, it turned out to be the *colour* of light that made all the difference. Bright red light? No effect. Dull blue light? Off the charge went.

This was a calamity. Everyone knew that the mathematical understanding of waves was rock solid, and yet there was nothing wrong with the experiment either. It was repeated all over the world and the same results kept appearing. The light was just not doing what it was supposed to do: it wasn't behaving like a wave. And, with that fact, the Knight lost his first arm.

Blow Number Two: The Problem of Infinite Energy

Elsewhere, at the same time, a second problem had arisen. Nobel Prize winner and discover of argon Lord Rayleigh (1842–1919) and his colleague Sir James Jeans (1877–1946) had been studying a particular type of object, one known as a "black body". They had calculated the number and type of light waves that a black body would emit when hot. The duo had produced some successful work on sound waves already, and applied similar ideas here.

There was some good news. For light of longer wavelengths, such as Hertz's radio waves, the new "Rayleigh–Jeans law" was in exact agreement with the measurements. The bad news, though, was very bad indeed. The law's predictions for what would happen with shorter waves, such as those of ultraviolet light, was ridiculous: it stated that impossibly huge amounts of energy would be pumped out of the hot body. So much so, in fact, that it said the emitted energy would actually be *infinite*.

This was clearly absurd: by this logic, even a lukewarm oven would kill us all off. Yet if light really was a series of continuous ripples, as was thought, the Rayleigh–Jeans infinite-energy prediction should stand. So worrying was this state of affairs that the physics community at the time referred to it as the "ultraviolet catastrophe". It was a deeply damaging strike: the second arm was off.

Blow Number Three: The Problem of the Destruction of Our Entire Universe

Our third nightmare finds its origins in the work of probably the finest experimentalist of them all, the brash New Zealander Ernest Rutherford (1871–1937). He had an uncanny knack for knowing what to try out in the lab and devised some of the best-engineered physics tests ever conducted. Having taken an interest in the rather fashionable "alpha particles" – which had been recently identified in the study of radioactivity – he decided to see what would happen if they were launched, at very high speed, towards unimaginably thin sheets of gold foil.

This could have been seen as a very odd decision. If the current understanding of atomic structure had been correct, the entire undertaking would have been a complete waste of time. The eminent J.J. Thomson (1856–1940) had experimentally determined that atoms must be made of some sort of positively charged "dough", with negatively charged particles called "electrons" embedded within it. The resulting solid lump was affectionately known as the "plum pudding model".

If Thomson was right (and everyone thought he was), Rutherford's data would have been uninteresting: the alpha particles would pass straight through the gold foil like the Black Knight's hot broadsword through butter. In the event, though, Rutherford's almost mystical instincts were rewarded. Some of the particles did the unthinkable: they bounced back. In his own words:

> It was quite the most incredible event that has ever happened to me in my life. It was almost as incredible as if you fired a 15-inch shell at a piece of tissue paper and it came back and hit you.[7]

A former student of J.J. Thomson, Rutherford had now rendered his ex-teacher's plum pudding model wholly incorrect. In its place, he devised the "nuclear model", one in which the positive charge was not spread out like dough, but was all concentrated in a tiny central "nucleus".

Rutherford's electrons were not embedded, but were instead found orbiting this nucleus, like planets orbit the Sun. This updated picture matched his data from the gold-foil tests and was later accepted as being the true view of the atom. All this could, and indeed should, be seen as quite a triumph. Once again, however, trouble was only a small wave-theory-sized step away, thanks to yet another (real-life) Knight of the Realm.

Sir Joseph Larmor (1857–1942) was an extremely talented mathematician. As an undergraduate, he had outscored all of his contemporaries at Cambridge University to be named "Senior Wrangler", the mathematical top dog. To put this into perspective, J.J. Thomson and James Clerk Maxwell, both now of legendary status, had finished their stints as "Second Wrangler", one rung down from Larmor.

In 1897, Larmor produced another calculation, this time to do with the light waves that would be given off by any moving charged particle. His findings quickly showed that something, somewhere was desperately wrong in our understanding for, when applied to

Rutherford's new nuclear model of the atom, the results are nothing short of cataclysmic.

Larmor showed that Rutherford's orbiting electrons would emit all of their energy, in the form of light waves, in just a fraction of a second. Doing so would cause them to spiral violently inwards towards the central nucleus, crash into it, and collapse the atom entirely. Matter, as we know it, would not exist. Our world – and us with it – would be completely and irretrievably gone. Needless to say, it was not looking at all good for our Black Knight's legs.

Decision Time

All in all, physics now found itself in a perplexing state. The first half of the nineteenth century had seen an explosion of knowledge about electromagnetism. James Clerk Maxwell had bound all of this up into a neat package, which was both theoretically striking and supported by experiment. Now three further experimental results had led to three absurd contradictions.

The wave theory of light was just not behaving itself properly; sometimes it seemed obedient to the physics community and at other times it threatened to obliterate the entirety of creation. It was beginning to look like resolving all this would mean tearing up the hard-won rulebook and starting all over again.

Just like the Black Knight, the electromagnetic-field-and-wave system had initially conquered all before it with ease. Suddenly, in a series of swift and deadly blows, it had been rendered limbless, just as he had. Now it was decision time. What should the scientists do?

Should they take the Black Knight's approach? Should they deny that there was any problem, plough on with their previously successful beliefs, and claim invincibility in the face of defeat?

After all, no one was actually physically hurt. The theory–experiment clashes weren't holding back the ongoing Industrial Revolution and they weren't affecting everyday life. Could these contradictions really be considered catastrophes when the only thing at stake was a genuine understanding of the world? Or is deeper wisdom about nature something worth fighting for?

Tiny Steps Forward

In the same decade that Maxwell wrote his equations, a teenager in Munich had become interested in physics. His teacher warned him against going any further with it, saying, "In this field, almost everything is already discovered, and all that remains is to fill a few holes."[8] Undeterred, this young man decided that filling holes might be enough for him, so he took up a place at university in the subject. Doing so would eventually bring his name – Planck – into physics classrooms worldwide.

Max Planck (1858–1947) chose to take on the infinite-energy problem of black body radiation; and he did so backwards. Instead of using wave theory to predict energy values, he started with the real energy measurements from the actual experiment, and then looked for maths that would predict those – even if that maths made no practical sense whatsoever.

Planck's aim was to end up with a set of numbers, produced by a formula, which matched the experimental results. He didn't appear to be interested in making any real-world claims about light, he just wanted the maths to work. This meant he could use a trial-and-error approach: just keep on tweaking the equation until the data it gives look like the real thing.

In the finalized – and working – version, Planck's light did not behave at all like that of traditional electromagnetism. Crudely put, his formula treated light as if it was emitted in tiny little chunks, one at a time, rather than as a smooth continuous wave. He introduced a number, now called the "Planck constant", which effectively split light energy into these chunks and determined how big they would be.

The maths worked very well indeed, but it was not at all clear what it actually meant – if anything at all. Planck himself saw his work as only a temporary and entirely fictional fix for the black body problem. As it turned out, though, it was far more than that. His disappearingly small constant would soon lead to the solutions of the two other "catastrophes" – thanks to some outside-the-box thinking from one of the all-time greats.

A Quantum Leap

It is very hard to find any area of twentieth-century physics which has not been significantly influenced by Albert Einstein. He now strides onto the stage of our play, as if to save the world by means of an outrageous and unjustifiable plot twist. And quite a twist it turns out to be.

Einstein took Planck's formula – a mathematical invention designed to generate the needed results – and treated it as if it were in fact a true description of nature. In what could reasonably be considered an utterly ridiculous move, he decided to work with the idea that light actually *did* come in chunks. These chunks became known as "quanta" – hence "quantum physics". In fact, he extended the idea further, claiming that light should no longer be thought of as a wave but as quanta travelling through space – as *particles*.

What makes this even more remarkable is that Einstein, in building his light-particle model, did not have the electromagnetic paradoxes as his main target. Instead he was motivated more by his work in the related field of thermodynamics, in which he had developed the belief that he needed to be able to somehow "count" light – an idea which desperately needed some other scientific justification. In Planck's "chunky" equation, Einstein had found what he was looking for: it gave him the perfect excuse to count light.

By taking Planck literally, Einstein had blown the wave theory of light out of the water. With light travelling as a particle instead, the curious photoelectric effect could be explained in full. In Einstein's new system, it was the *colour* of the light that determined how much energy a light particle had rather than its brightness.

A blue light particle – or "photon" – had high energy, whereas a red photon had low energy. A blue photon could therefore release a negatively charged electron from a metal; a red photon couldn't. Making the light *brighter* in Einstein's world simply meant sending *more* photons in towards the charge, which would not change the outcome: photons only operated one at a time, so sending in extra low-energy red ones would just mean more failed attempts. Even the brightest red light imaginable would not release electrons. Blue light, no matter how dim, would. The puzzle was solved.

The electron-energy-death-spiral issue, Larmor's finding that atoms should almost instantaneously collapse in on themselves, was also fixed using Planck's "quantized" light. Niels Bohr (1885–1962) adapted Einstein's insights to suggest a different structure of the atom. In his model, the electrons only ever orbited in fixed circles of different sizes; no spiralling inwards or outwards was allowed. Electrons could instead "hop" directly from one orbit-circle to another by taking in or getting rid of energy, but only if that energy was in whole Planck-sized chunks.

With Bohr's electrons not able to lose energy as a continuous wave-like stream, and therefore not able to spiral, the problem disappeared. The jumping-between-fixed-circles picture of the atom simply banned any idea of electrons sliding in towards the nucleus; the smallest circle was as close to the nucleus as the electron was ever allowed to be. Because of this, the atom was unable to collapse. The universe was saved.

A Weird New World

By 1913, then, the apparent paradoxes of the photoelectric effect, black body radiation, and atomic destruction had all been resolved. The new "quantum mechanics" began to take over. The more it was investigated, the weirder it seemed, and yet it grew in explanatory power on a scale that no theory before it had ever begun to approach. Quantum mechanics did not behave like any of its predecessors; it was not intuitive at all and kept on producing findings that hovered right on the very edge of the impossible.

For example, it was soon shown that an electron could be in more than one place at the same time. Also, electrons could "teleport". Certain particles, the new science said, could pile up on each other in limitless numbers, while others were held apart for ever. As if this wasn't enough, experiment and theory both showed that an electron could spread itself out as it travelled through tiny gaps, forming a sort of blurry electron-smudge, which then reassembled into a particle at the end of its journey. It seemed that order and common sense had been thrown out of the window. As Bohr stated: "Those who are not shocked when they first come across quantum theory cannot possibly have understood it."[9]

To add to this madness, Werner Heisenberg (1901–76) showed that if you knew where a particle was located, you could *not* know how fast it was going, and vice versa. Known as the "uncertainty principle", his maths also allows for particles to suddenly "pop" into existence out of nothing, provided they then disappear again quickly enough.

This new world was unrecognizable. The equations and experiments were leading physicists and mathematicians to conclusions about our existence that no one, even the most imaginative of thinkers, would have ever suggested – other than Grosseteste in the thirteenth century, of course.

The scientific community had made the bold decision to press on for deeper wisdom, to go wherever the evidence led, no matter what the consequences were for previously cherished theories. And, in doing so, they had been rewarded in the most spectacular and unexpected of ways.

Saving the Baby

One last development needs mentioning before we can begin our study of faith and its relevance to our discussion. Having thrown out some of the old electromagnetic bathwater, it was still necessary to deal with the fact that much of it had actually worked very well. Was there, perhaps, a baby to be saved?

The rescue began when Louis de Broglie (1892–1987) made a seemingly outrageous suggestion in 1924: that all particles could, under certain conditions, be thought of as *waves*. At first blush, this would appear to be the ravings of a madman, but two key facts can help us see that it might not be quite as crazy as it sounds.

First, the argument of whether light was a wave or a particle went back far further even than Newton who, incidentally, was on the particle side of the debate. Second, the quirky nature of quantum mechanics now meant that anyone could put any physics idea forward without too much fear of ridicule.

De Broglie used some of Einstein's ideas about photons to justify his work. If these light-particles had somehow tricked people into thinking they were waves, he reasoned, then why shouldn't other particles, such as electrons, have done the same? Within three years of his announcement, electron-waves were indeed found in lab experiments.

Following on from de Broglie, Erwin Schrödinger (1887–1961) decided to go the whole hog. He put together an ingenious equation that described whole systems of particles using wave mathematics, and this new way of thinking led to the most accurate predictions of physical behaviour ever made in the entire history of science.

The dividing line between wave and particle, previously considered an impenetrable wall, was now so far beyond blurred that it barely existed. Particle theory could be applied to waves. Wave theory could be applied to particles. Both approaches were sometimes right; both were sometimes wrong. But when the two were brought together in this new, hybridized form, it all worked – brilliantly.

Chasing Down Deep Wisdom

At the start of our story, the invention of the battery led to the linking of electricity, magnetism and light in a hugely successful light-wave theory. Upsettingly, some experimental results then threatened to undermine the whole system. In their determination to follow the facts, however, scientists started thinking about physics in an entirely new and exotic way: quantum mechanics.

Eventually, by bringing wave and particle behaviour together, it was shown that the sometimes-wave-and-sometimes-particle theory could explain the whole show. Back to Einstein:

> But what is light really? Is it a wave or a shower of photons?
> … It seems as though we must use sometimes the one theory
> and sometimes the other, while at times we may use either…
> separately neither of them fully explains the phenomena of light,
> but together they do.[10]

This is science at its very best. Grasping hold of both their innate ability and their belief that the world would yield up answers (see Chapter 3), this century-and-a-half of searchers chased down wisdom about nature. When they found themselves confronted with contradictions, they were prepared to change their minds and follow the evidence where it led. They were not satisfied when they unearthed a mismatch between their ideas and reality, even though the consequences for everyday life at the time were minimal.

Eventually, through their reason and their imaginations, they cracked one of the strangest cases of all. Nature gave up its secrets. And, as it did, it was clear that wisdom about our universe – at its most fundamental level – was far, far deeper than any one of them would have ever dreamt. Is there still more we can we learn from this start-again story? We have seen that the call to understand the natural world in a new way can be traced right back to Job, but can an understanding of biblical Christianity shed any light on the process of scientific revolution? If so, how?

Can Faith-Heads Change Their Minds?

We have seen the glory of science in its readiness to change theory to fit facts. Yet it has become a popular notion, mainly due to a few key figures popularizing it, that when science follows the evidence it is doing something that faith does not – and cannot – do. Sometimes, the assertion goes even further than that and suggests that faith is happiest when it operates *against* evidence.

It is a favoured line of attack for Richard Dawkins, whom we encountered in our opening chapter. In his book *The Selfish Gene* we find the fairly well-known line about faith, something which he says "… means blind trust, in the absence of evidence, even in the teeth of evidence".[11]

His is a clear message: science carefully and correctly treasures *facts*, even if that means starting all over again, while faith rejoices in holding on to *unsupported belief*, especially if it seems that all the signs are pointing the other way. Dawkins utilizes this approach again in his more recent work, *The God Delusion*:

> If this book works as intended, religious readers who open it
> will be atheists when they put it down. What presumptuous
> optimism! Of course, dyed-in-the-wool faith-heads are immune
> to argument, their resistance built up over the years of childhood
> indoctrination using methods that took centuries to mature.[12]

This claim that "faith-heads" are immune to argument is, as would undoubtedly please Dawkins, one which can be tested: we can look at the facts available, and decide whether it is right or wrong. We can ask, for example, whether biblical Christianity has anything to say about responding to mismatches between evidence and belief.

We can ask if it provides models of how to think afresh in the light of new information. We can ask if it calls on its adherents to chase down truth and, if necessary, change their minds – even if that means letting go of deep but incorrect convictions. When we have done so we will find that, for the Christian, evidence is not something to be ignored or dismissed at all: it is to be greatly treasured and acted upon.

The Value of Wisdom

From beginning to end, the Bible is written to be a celebration of the extraordinary greatness of the three-in-one God. Father, Son, and Spirit are exalted as being perfectly good, ultimately powerful, and comprehensively in charge of the created universe. Whenever there is the danger of someone or something else being praised instead, the point is hammered home that only God is to be worshipped.

There are warnings against bowing down to earthly rulers, to man-made idols, and even to angels, as we see here at the end of John's Revelation:

> I, John, am the one who heard and saw these things. And when I had heard and seen them, I fell down to worship at the feet of the angel who had been showing them to me. But he said to me, "Don't do that! I am a fellow servant with you and with your fellow prophets and with all who keep the words of this scroll. Worship God!"[13]

The righteousness of serving God alone is not lost on Job either: he is aware of yet another competitor for our affections – nature itself. He has made efforts to avoid falling this way:

> If I have regarded the sun in its radiance
> or the moon moving in splendour,
> so that my heart was secretly enticed
> and my hand offered them a kiss of homage,
> then these also would be sins to be judged,
> for I would have been unfaithful to God on high.[14]

The Bible, therefore, is very careful to guard God's uniqueness and holiness. As a result, it often seeks to minimize even the grandest aspects of his creation. Given this, we could perhaps be taken aback at the kind of language used in Proverbs when discussing *wisdom*:

> The Lord brought me forth as the first of his works,
> before his deeds of old;
> I was formed long ages ago,
> at the very beginning, when the world came to be.
> When there were no watery depths, I was given birth,
> when there were no springs overflowing with water;
> before the mountains were settled in place,
> before the hills, I was given birth,
> before he made the world or its fields
> or any of the dust of the earth.
> I was there when he set the heavens in place,
> when he marked out the horizon on the face of the deep,
> when he established the clouds above
> and fixed securely the fountains of the deep,
> when he gave the sea its boundary

so that the waters would not overstep his command,
and when he marked out the foundations of the earth.
Then I was constantly at his side.
I was filled with delight day after day,
rejoicing always in his presence,
rejoicing in his whole world
and delighting in the human race.[15]

The fact that wisdom is talked about like a real person is close to astonishing, since it opens up the possibility of wisdom itself being worshipped as a deity. The Bible does not run a risk like this lightly. For it to talk about wisdom in this way tells us that it is to be thought of as something incredibly valuable – below God himself, of course, but right at the top of everything that has been created. This is reinforced by other verses from the same passage:

Does not wisdom call out?
Does not understanding raise her voice?
At the highest point along the way,
where the paths meet, she takes her stand;
beside the gate leading into the city,
at the entrance, she cries aloud:
"To you, O people, I call out;
I raise my voice to all humanity.
You who are simple, gain prudence;
you who are foolish, set your hearts on it.
Listen, for I have trustworthy things to say;
I open my lips to speak what is right.
My mouth speaks what is true,
for my lips detest wickedness.
All the words of my mouth are just;
none of them is crooked or perverse.
To the discerning all of them are right;
they are upright to those who have found knowledge.
Choose my instruction instead of silver,
knowledge rather than choice gold,
for wisdom is more precious than rubies,
and nothing you desire can compare with her."[16]

If the Bible were indeed a book designed to shut down the mind, we would not expect to find texts like this one within it. Here, the instruction is to seek out truth, which is *more precious than rubies*. Deep wisdom about our circumstances and about our world is promoted just about as highly as anything in the created realm could be.

It is clear from this that the believer is to pursue truth diligently and to enjoy doing so. The Christian is instructed to learn, not to shut out knowledge. Far from being a community that runs away from investigation – from development, new information, or science – the church is to be at the forefront of finding out what can be found out.

Granted, this is no complete answer yet. One could certainly complain that the passage above is nothing to do with evidence or theory or changing your mind. What exactly does the author of Proverbs mean by *wisdom*, anyway? Are there any concrete examples of start-again stories – of mind-changes – available in Christian Scripture? If so, what can we learn from them?

The Wrong Timescale

The Old Testament book of Psalms is full of emotional outbursts. These include rants about worldly injustice, laments about the pains of depression, songs about the joy of knowing God, and grand hymns about his majesty. The whole range of emotions is present and there is no censorship to be seen. It is in this book that we will find our first example of a start-again story.

As is the case with the rest of the Bible, Psalms is a real-world text that does not cover up the difficult things of life or hide the anger or despair with which we naturally respond. In Psalm 73, for example, we find someone called Asaph caught up in both agony and frustration with what he sees around him.

Asaph initially declares his belief in the goodness of God; but then lays out his struggles at the contradictory reality he is actually living in:

> Surely God is good to Israel,
> to those who are pure in heart.
> But as for me, my feet had almost slipped;
> I had nearly lost my foothold.
> For I envied the arrogant
> when I saw the prosperity of the wicked.
>
> They have no struggles;
> their bodies are healthy and strong.

They are free from common human burdens;
they are not plagued by human ills.
Therefore pride is their necklace;
they clothe themselves with violence.
From their callous hearts comes iniquity;
their evil imaginations have no limits.
They scoff, and speak with malice;
with arrogance they threaten oppression.
Their mouths lay claim to heaven,
and their tongues take possession of the earth.
Therefore their people turn to them
and drink up waters in abundance.
They say, "How would God know?
Does the Most High know anything?"
This is what the wicked are like –
always free of care, they go on amassing wealth.

Surely in vain I have kept my heart pure
and have washed my hands in innocence.
All day long I have been afflicted,
and every morning brings new punishments.[17]

Asaph is miserable. Those around him, who happily ignore God, seem to be thriving. He, in the meantime, has served God; and yet he is suffering. This is blatantly unfair. Or at least, Asaph thinks it is, because he has held, so far, to a particular theory of divine justice.

This theory says that God is righteous and loves righteousness, so will reward it. Similarly, God hates cruelty and evil, so he will punish it. It is a simple yet sensible model, found elsewhere in ancient writings, including Job. Believing it to be true, Asaph has committed himself to God. The problem is this: his theory doesn't match the facts. He is being good and others aren't; yet he is losing out and they are doing just fine. This is Asaph's own real-life ultraviolet catastrophe. What should he do?

If Dawkins is right, then Asaph – who is a faith-head – will keep on believing the same old thing. If Dawkins is right, then the fact that Asaph's beliefs are out of line with what he sees will actually encourage him to maintain them, because that is what faith *does*. At this point, however, a good scientist would change their theory. What, then, will Asaph do?

When I tried to understand all this,
it troubled me deeply
till I entered the sanctuary of God;
then I understood their final destiny.

Surely you place them on slippery ground;
you cast them down to ruin.
How suddenly are they destroyed,
completely swept away by terrors!
They are like a dream when one awakes;
when you arise, Lord,
you will despise them as fantasies.

When my heart was grieved
and my spirit embittered,
I was senseless and ignorant;
I was a brute beast before you.

Yet I am always with you;
you hold me by my right hand.
You guide me with your counsel,
and afterwards you will take me into glory.
Whom have I in heaven but you?
And earth has nothing I desire besides you.
My flesh and my heart may fail,
but God is the strength of my heart
and my portion for ever.

Those who are far from you will perish;
you destroy all who are unfaithful to you.
But as for me, it is good to be near God.
I have made the Sovereign Lord my refuge;
I will tell of all your deeds.[18]

First, it should be noted that Asaph *tried to understand all this*. Blind faith would not have done so. Blind faith would suppress the mismatch, or wish it away. Yet Asaph pushes on, searching out the deeper wisdom that will resolve his contradiction – just as the quantum pioneers did. And he finds it. He had been wrong after all. His belief that God blesses the righteous and punishes the wicked was correct, but he had added an incorrect assumption to it, resulting in a broken theory.

Asaph had wrongly imagined that God would do all of this during the lifetime of the individuals. It is only when he delves further – enters God's sanctuary – that the truth comes to him. God will certainly ensure that justice is done, but on a different timescale altogether: that of eternity.

Asaph now understands that his previous simplistic earthly conviction made him like a *brute beast*. His God is not required to bless him now: God will take him *into glory*, which is better by far. The circumstances on earth that were breaking Asaph's heart suddenly seems a lot smaller; his perspective has changed, thanks to a glimpse of eternal reality.

It is important to understand the point here: there is no claim being made that this psalm is science, or that this is scientific thinking. It is not relevant to current argument whether or not Asaph is correct in his thoughts – or even whether he, or his God, exist. What matters is this: the Bible is presenting – positively – a case in which someone believed something deeply, was confronted with a contradiction and then changed their beliefs.

This is exactly the same pattern as we saw with our twentieth-century scientists; the psalmist got there two-and-half millennia earlier. Asaph is a faith-head who has changed his mind. He has lived out his own start-again story. And he is not the only one.

The End of the Way

In the earliest days of Christianity – when the believers were still numbered in thousands and located in a relatively small region around Jerusalem – there existed a very real danger of the faith being eliminated completely. This was due to the beliefs and methods of just one man: Saul of Tarsus.

Trained in the understanding of the Jewish writings by the very best teachers and gifted with an extraordinary mind, Saul (AD 5–67) had come to the conclusion that the followers of Jesus were not just harmlessly deluded: they were dangerous. This was not because of any observable violent tendencies among them, but because he thought their worshipping of Jesus as God was blasphemous.

Saul was worried. If this new movement was to gain any more momentum (it had grown with amazing speed), many more people might be led astray. In joining the "Way", as it was then called, they would dishonour the true God of Israel, bringing woe onto themselves and their land. Saul, in taking this view, committed himself to the only course of action which seemed right to him: the utter destruction of the church.

He oversaw the stoning of Stephen, a key member of the Jerusalem congregation, and triggered a major outbreak of persecution against Christians, many fleeing for their lives. Not satisfied yet, we then read in the New Testament book, Acts of the Apostles, that:

> Saul was still breathing out murderous threats against the Lord's disciples. He went to the high priest and asked him for letters to the synagogues in Damascus, so that if he found any there who belonged to the Way, whether men or women, he might take them as prisoners to Jerusalem.[19]

A fierce, intense, and highly intelligent man, Saul was totally convinced that his beliefs were correct. They were, after all, the result of much study and much thought over many years. The emergence of the Way horrified him. It was all very clear to Saul: Jesus was a fraud. His followers were spitting in the face of God. Christianity was the despicable act of worshipping a human being; allegiance to it was punishable by prison or death.

This set of principles had become Saul's own personal Black Knight, and the ground he gained in Jerusalem served as an important early victory. There is little doubt that Saul's certainty and drive meant he would not stop until the job was done. In fact, without a King Arthur moment, Saul might well have finished off the Jesus story before the first Gospel had even been written. On the way to Damascus, however, this moment arrived and, fittingly, it was to be an encounter with a king.

The Greatest Mind-Change in History

Later on in his life, Saul found himself in a great deal of trouble with the Jewish establishment – and, in turn, the Roman authorities. He was accused of inciting riots, of blasphemous behaviour, and of causing social, political, and religious upheaval. In one of his many trials, he was given the opportunity to speak his case before Herod Agrippa II, king in Jerusalem, in around AD 59. This was not the first time Saul had been in the presence of a royal figure. In fact, as he goes on to explain, a far more significant Ruler had met with him, years ago, on the Damascus road. We join him at the start of his speech:

King Agrippa, I consider myself fortunate to stand before you today as I make my defence against all the accusations of the Jews, and especially so because you are well acquainted with all the Jewish customs and controversies. Therefore, I beg you to listen to me patiently.

The Jewish people all know the way I have lived ever since I was a child, from the beginning of my life in my own country, and also in Jerusalem. They have known me for a long time and can testify, if they are willing, that I conformed to the strictest sect of our religion, living as a Pharisee…

I too was convinced that I ought to do all that was possible to oppose the name of Jesus of Nazareth. And that is just what I did in Jerusalem. On the authority of the chief priests I put many of the Lord's people in prison, and when they were put to death, I cast my vote against them. Many a time I went from one synagogue to another to have them punished, and I tried to force them to blaspheme. I was so obsessed with persecuting them that I even hunted them down in foreign cities.

On one of these journeys I was going to Damascus with the authority and commission of the chief priests. About noon, King Agrippa, as I was on the road, I saw a light from heaven, brighter than the sun, blazing around me and my companions. We all fell to the ground, and I heard a voice saying to me in Aramaic, "Saul, Saul, why do you persecute me? It is hard for you to kick against the goads."

Then I asked, "Who are you, Lord?"

"I am Jesus, whom you are persecuting," the Lord replied.[20]

This changed everything for Saul. His previous theory – that Jesus was merely a man who had spawned a repulsive cult – was torn apart in the teeth of this new evidence. Saul's Black Knight was dismembered by the sudden revelation of this heavenly king. His account continues, explaining that he was then completely turned around by Jesus: rather than persecuting the followers of the Way, Saul would become its main mouthpiece. As he goes on to say:

So then, King Agrippa, I was not disobedient to the vision from heaven. First to those in Damascus, then to those in Jerusalem and in all Judea, and then to the Gentiles, I preached that they should repent and turn to God and demonstrate their repentance by their deeds.[21]

This new Saul chose to be known as "Paul" – changing his name from one with rich kingly heritage to a new one that verged on slang and meant "small". He dedicated the rest of his life to taking the news about Jesus far and wide; setting up churches in multiple cities and writing letters that now form a large chunk of the New Testament. As he explains all of this to the court, he gets an unsurprising response from Festus, a Roman official:

> "You are out of your mind, Paul!" he shouted. "Your great learning is driving you insane."[22]

Well aware of the extraordinary nature of his story, Paul seeks to reassure him that his convictions are not all pie in the sky; they are the product of proper analysis of real evidence:

> "I am not insane, most excellent Festus," Paul replied. "What I am saying is true and reasonable."[23]

Paul's utter about-face must have come from somewhere. After all, he went from murdering Christians to risking his life to spread Christianity. The writings he goes on to produce are well reasoned, logical, carefully argued, and call others to change their minds – *repent* – just as he has done. Paul is a man who is interested in following the facts wherever they lead, and he has become convinced that they lead to Jesus being the Almighty Creator God. He and Asaph are faith-heads, certainly. Yet when they had their views of reality challenged by the evidence, they changed them – just as all biblical wisdom-seekers should.

Science and Repenting

As we have seen in this chapter, there are times in science when a theory is called into question by new discoveries. The correct response to this is to change the theory – if necessary, to change it completely – even if it has been elegant, dearly loved and successful up until that point. This is the calling on scientists: follow the evidence.

We have also seen that a few observers have suggested – quite strongly at times – that people of faith are unprepared to follow this same call. Undoubtedly, this is true of some Christians some of the time. When it is, however, those individuals are not really living up to the challenges and patterns laid out in the Bible. In actuality, the Bible is a book that tells us repeatedly of the need to seek out resolutions to contradictions. It tells us of the need to change our minds in the face of the truth. It tells us of the need to *repent*.

More than that, it says that it is not possible to be a biblical Christian at all unless you have changed your mind about reality completely. So drastic is this change that it is described as being like an entirely new life. Jesus himself tells an enquirer that entering the kingdom of heaven is like being "born again". As Paul says in two of his letters to Christian churches:

Be transformed by the renewing of your mind.[24]

You were taught, with regard to your former way of life, to put off your old self, which is being corrupted by its deceitful desires; to be made new in the attitude of your minds.[25]

Biblical repentance depends on the realization that, up until this point, the repenter has been completely wrong, and that it is time to face the facts. There is another name for this process of mind-change: "conversion". Some conversions are dramatic, like Saul/Paul's. Some are more low-key, and some are even unenthusiastic. Take the renowned Oxford academic C.S. Lewis (1898–1963) for an example of the latter:

You must picture me alone in that room in Magdalen, night after night, feeling, whenever my mind lifted even for a second from my work, the steady, unrelenting approach of Him whom I so earnestly desired not to meet. That which I greatly feared had at last come upon me. In the Trinity Term of 1929 I gave in, and admitted that God was God, and knelt and prayed: perhaps, that night, the most dejected and reluctant convert in all England.[26]

This process of conversion gives converts a great advantage when it comes to changing their mind in other circumstances. Rather than faith-heads being people immune to argument, they should be people who have already overhauled their thinking to a greater extent than anyone else has, for they have changed their entire worldview.

Therefore, when a scientist with a grounding in the Christian faith finds themselves faced with a potential scientific revolution, they are well equipped; they have already experienced a personal revolution of even larger magnitude. Starting again in *science* will be easier for someone who has already started again in *life*. It should come as no surprise, then, that many of the great names mentioned in the science start-again story of this chapter are themselves converts.

Scientific and Personal Revolutions

When he introduced the radical idea of electromagnetic fields, Michael Faraday unlocked a whole new area of physics to be explored, much of which is still being used today. Rather than his Christianity getting in the way of his ability to think about new ideas, he saw science as a way of developing familiarity with God's work and so enjoying it all the more:

> I cannot doubt that a glorious discovery in natural knowledge, and the wisdom and power of God in the creation, is awaiting our age, and that we may not only hope to see it, but even be honoured to help in obtaining the victory over present ignorance and future knowledge.[27]

Likewise, James Clerk Maxwell – the man who made the light-wave breakthrough that moved even Einstein – saw his scientific work as a calling to go alongside his personal decision to follow Jesus:

> I think men of science as well as other men need to learn from Christ, and I think Christians whose minds are scientific are bound to study science that their view of the glory of God may be as extensive as their being is capable.[28]

Max Planck, the inventor of the constant that ushered in a new age and triggered the quantum takeover, viewed his faith as the bedrock on which his science was built:

> Both religion and science require a belief in God. For believers, God is in the beginning, and for physicists He is at the end of all considerations… To the former He is the foundation, to the latter, the crown.[29]

Werner Heisenberg was awarded the Nobel Prize in 1932 "for the creation of quantum mechanics", the bizarre new science which demanded repentance from older models. He claimed, as we would have to agree, that following the facts was the key – and he extended this principle further, drawing even deeper conclusions:

The first gulp from the glass of natural sciences will turn you into
an atheist, but at the bottom of the glass God is waiting for you.[30]

In Chapter 3, we saw that the Christian faith provides a firm basis for
pursuing science. It does this by stating that God has given us both
scientific capability and a universe which will give up its truth. In
this chapter, we see that it also provides – in the need for repentance
– the ultimate model of how to change your mind in the light of the
evidence.

In powerfully exultant language, the Bible calls us to treasure
wisdom greatly. It calls us to seek it out wherever it may be found
and to change our theories in the face of new realization. It calls
us to repent of old and mistaken beliefs and to "be transformed by
the renewing of our minds". In so doing, it prepares the scientist
to undertake, if necessary, a complete revision of what is true; for
Christianity tells the start-again story to *begin* all others.

5

PAIN, SUFFERING, AND HOPE

Science is difficult and slow no matter who you are. The hours are long, and the glorious "aha" days come only very infrequently. You have to keep believing that if you put in the hours, those days will indeed come!

Bonnie Bassler

As you know, we count as blessed those who have persevered.

The apostle James

The science stories that we have looked at so far – peptides, pomegranates, photons – could well give the impression that science always marches on forwards with no missed steps. Is that an accurate picture? Does science sometimes fail? Is it sometimes messy, difficult, or even painful? Does it hold within it the same gritty realism we encountered in Asaph's psalm? To help answer these questions, yet another story – that of an unfortunate obstetrician – is worth our consideration; and not much of it is pleasant.

Ignaz Semmelweis (1818–65) was a Hungarian doctor specializing in childbirth and aftercare for new mothers and babies. In 1846, he was appointed to a senior role at Vienna General Hospital, an institution which, he noticed, had a bizarre and dreadful problem. It seemed that the more its doctors got involved in helping a woman, the more likely she was to die.

During the first year of his tenure, the "First Clinic" – the one attended to by doctors and medical students – saw more than one in ten of the mothers pass away. Semmelweis observed that this was over four times worse than the lower-profile "Second Clinic", which was midwife-run; and it was over twenty times worse than the overall figures from the same hospital thirty years earlier.

This was hardly news to the general populace, however, who were already well aware of the dismal state of things. In fact, the situation was so shocking that pregnant women in Vienna had begun choosing to give birth in the street, rather than run the risk of facing a doctor.

Semmelweis rightly decided that all this needed to be properly investigated. Studying historical statistics on childbirth, he noticed two major patterns. First, the mortality rate of the mothers had suddenly skyrocketed in 1823, the same year that medical studies of dead bodies had been introduced to the hospital. Second, the difference between the death rates on the two clinics had only appeared in 1841, the year that the doctor–midwife separation had been brought in.

These two insights led to a conclusion: Semmelweis became convinced that the problem was doctors working on corpses. He guessed that something in the "dead" material on their hands was making the women they then attended become desperately ill.

Backing his hunch, Semmelweis made it hospital policy for all medical students and doctors involved in autopsies to wash their hands before going on to treat a patient. The effect was instantaneous. In the year after handwashing, the number of young mothers dying dropped more than tenfold. Hundreds of lives were saved.

So far, this reads like yet another cut-and-dried scientific success story – but it isn't. In a disastrous development, Semmelweis's work actually managed to upset people. Specifically, it upset some influential doctors, who felt offended at the suggestion that their hands might be contaminated.

Dr Charles Meigs (1792–1869), working in obstetrics in America, strongly contested the dirty-hand accusation in a series of writings. He is claimed to have said, "Doctors are gentlemen, and gentlemen's hands are always clean." While the exact wording of the quote cannot be verified, it is certainly a fair summary of his position.[1] Sadly, Meigs's views were shared by many. As well as this, there were more than a few physicians who were simply sceptical that cleanliness could even matter.

Semmelweis was challenged to produce proof, but he couldn't. The tiny microorganisms which were transmitting infection were invisible, and there was no room for them in the science of the day. Although he had statistics to support his methods, he was unable to provide a conclusive *explanation* for their existence.

Even though handwashing had brought about the most dramatic of improvements, few other hospitals or doctors across Europe or America followed suit, and women kept dying from infection after childbirth at alarming rates. In the absence of a neatly packaged, well-evidenced biological theory, Semmelweis found himself doubted and eventually ostracized.

Despite the new mortality rate being its lowest for multiple decades, the Vienna hospital did not renew Semmelweis's contract when it expired in 1849, and his professional life never fully recovered from that. He continued to collect and study statistics on maternal deaths, pleading with doctors to support his case, but those who were set against him seemed to hold more sway. He was fighting what would prove to be – for him, and for many young women – a losing battle.

Over the next decade or so, Semmelweis developed a nervous disorder, began drinking heavily, and became utterly obsessed with the issue of death after childbirth, never letting it leave his mind. He wrote letters violently attacking his opponents, accusing them of ignorance and even murder for not taking up his theory. His behaviour became more and more desperate and, in 1865, he was referred to an asylum against his wishes.

Protesting against the decision, he was badly beaten by the guards, bound tightly, and thrown into isolation. Two weeks later, Semmelweis was dead, with the beating being the most likely cause. These brutal injuries to his body were to be quickly followed by equally brutal insults to his legacy.

The association of doctors to which he belonged traditionally held commemoration services for members, but Semmelweis received no such honour; they ignored his passing completely. In the fifteen years between his dismissal and his death, thousands of new mothers across Europe had died, unnecessarily, of infection. Ignaz Semmelweis, their potential saviour, lost his life in the same way so many of them did – without anybody really noticing.

This is a horribly sad story, and it is made worse by the sense of missed opportunity. The scientific process did not yield up to Semmelweis the proof he needed to convince his peers, no matter how hard he tried. The human cost was huge, on both individual and community levels. The Semmelweis tragedy is dramatic proof that pursuing science can sometimes be painful and difficult.

In this case, Semmelweis's intuitions were right – but pain in science can also be caused when our "best" ideas turn out to be wrong. Trying to follow facts can invite ridicule, it can fail, it can frustrate; and yet we persist. Why? Surely, the answer is *hope* – hope that answers will come, hope that truth will win out, hope that wisdom will reveal itself. Hope, ultimately, that the present struggle – however hard it may be – will be worth it.

In the remainder of this chapter, we will take a closer look at the struggles within science and the hopefulness that carries people through. We will ask if there is perhaps a bigger picture here, and how that might help the scientist. We will find, once again, that *faith* is best called upon to keep science going in its darkest moments. Faith brings the energy that is needed in our laboratories. Faith supplies the drive needed in our classrooms. Faith provides the hope needed in our hospitals.

Steiner's Saturday

In Chapter 1, we considered many varied views on what science is and what it is for. There, we heard George Steiner saying that we can sometimes feel deeply uncomfortable when we try to understand our universe – it can even spook us – because of the "inhuman otherness of matter".

Building on this theme, he puts forward the notion that the human experience is one of strange tension; we are all, somehow, *waiting* for something. According to Steiner, humanity finds itself deep inside a kind of in-between time: nothing really seems to make proper sense yet, but there is forever hope that it might.

To illustrate this point, Steiner (although not a Christian himself) chooses the three days of the Easter story, considering the emotions and qualities sewn into each one. *Friday* is the day that Jesus was executed; a day of disaster, of loss, of darkness and of confusion. *Sunday* is the day that Jesus is raised; it sings of victory, of love, of freedom and completion. Steiner's claim is that neither of these days is where we find ourselves:

> Ours is the long day's journey of the Saturday. Between suffering, aloneness, unutterable waste on the one hand and the dream of liberation and rebirth on the other.[2]

Steiner is using powerful and imaginative language to cry out what has been on the lips, or at least on the minds, of most people at some time or another: "Things just don't seem *right*!" The sense that life should be different somehow – that it should be *better* – seems almost universal. The Easter story is the story of all people. It is most certainly present in science.

Presenting science as the cold, logical activity of scientists who are devoid of emotional attachment, of personal investment, and of *hope* would be wholly inaccurate. As we saw with Semmelweis, real science can contain struggles against ignorance, against confusion, and against a world that can seem cruel, or even broken.

Without hope, science would be a miserable exercise. Fortunately, there does seem to be at least some of it about, and we shall illustrate this by dropping in on the biggest scientific quest of them all: the search for a Grand Unified Theory.

Laying Foundations

In Chapter 4, we saw something of the pivotal role that Albert Einstein played in the quantum revolution. Only a few people can claim to have initiated scientific revolutions, so Einstein's work would have already ensured his place in the history-of-science books. He did not rest on his light-particle laurels, though, and in 1915 he brought yet another giant to life. As was briefly mentioned in Chapter 3, Einstein formulated the extraordinary system of general relativity, and our understanding of the world would never be the same again.

At its heart, general relativity is mathematical; it consists of geometrical equations. The description it gives of the universe is so *visual*, however, that it has even been given *The Simpsons* treatment. It is therefore likely that the reader has come across one of its key concepts – that the vast realm of space we live in can be reimagined as a bendable, foldable rubbery sheet. But what does that actually mean? This is indeed a tough question. Let us begin our answer by thinking about how we can even ask it in the first place.

It is of ultimate importance in science (physics in particular) to agree on some sort of fundamental starting point: in effect, to decide what might be the "fixed" stage on which all the scientists are playing. Without this there can be no basis for comparing theories, or even measurements. Just as Euclid began with five assumptions without proving them, scientists also need to start somewhere.

To illustrate this point, let us imagine that two competing scientific ideas have been put forward by well-known, reliable institutions. Each idea seeks to explain the same body of facts, but upon further investigation a crucial difference is found. It turns out that the two ideas were built on different basic assumptions about reality.

It is impossible to judge between them without first studying which set of assumptions is the best. Once that is determined, at least one of the theories will require heavy editing, and may well have to be thrown out completely. For this reason, we need to agree from the very beginning on a set of assumptions, like Euclid. Our notion of a fixed stage really does matter if anyone is to give a performance of value.

Isaac Newton, when putting together his mathematical analysis of motion, discussed the twin concepts of "absolute space" and "absolute time". He believed that space was a rock-solid, unchangeable platform and that time rolled ever-faithfully forwards. In some senses, he thought of these absolutes as deeply mystical and unknowable; but believed they could be made use of nonetheless.

Newton assumed, for example, that both lengths and durations were *measurable* – lengths between two points in absolute space and durations between two points in absolute time. These measured values could then be used for calculations. He wrote about this when discussing the framework for his *Principia*, the masterpiece we touched upon in Chapter 2:

> Absolute true and mathematical time, of itself, and from its own nature flows equably without regard to anything external...
> Absolute space, in its own nature, without regard to anything external, remains always similar and immovable.[3]

Since both space and time could not be affected by anything else, they provided the fixed stage needed for his – and everybody else's – mathematical modelling of physics. Newton used them to derive his laws of motion, which became the go-to equations for anyone working in the same arena.

When combined with earlier insights from Galileo, it could be shown that Newton's resulting work had a very special property known as "invariance". Invariance is very important, because it means that the model can be used in a variety of different circumstances. Newton's laws worked when the experimenters using them were stationary and would also be correct if they were moving at a steady speed.

This has a rather surprising consequence. Consider a scientist on board an aeroplane that has blacked-out windows. She is asked whether the plane is flying through the air at 500 mph or still parked on the runway. Invariance states that all Newtonian experiments will work in both situations, so there is nothing she can do within the plane to find out. She can try dropping masses, bouncing balls, throwing darts, but the results in both situations are identical, so she is unable to answer the question.

It may not be immediately obvious, but this is actually a good thing. If a theory's results are unaffected by a potentially major factor like constant motion, then they are more powerful: they will be true in more situations. This is the kind of finding that helps lay the foundations needed for others to work with.

Newton had developed a reasonable starting point for physicists. Lengths, durations, laws of motion, and consistent behaviour in different sets of circumstances all feel like good solid ground. Einstein, though, had other ideas.

And You Thought Quantum Mechanics Was Weird?

If Newton's laws were the same for the moving and non-moving observer, thought Einstein, then what else in physics might be? Our scientist in the aeroplane was conducting seventeenth-century experiments like those of Galileo: rolling, dropping, or throwing things. Time, however, had moved on. Why couldn't she be doing something more modern? Why couldn't she be playing around with batteries, or alpha particles – or electromagnetism?

Einstein was already aware that Maxwell's equations had their own type of invariance. He used this knowledge to take a bold step: he decided to treat the speed of light as always being the same no matter who measured it. The scientist on the plane would therefore measure this value to be 300 million metres per second every single time, regardless of the plane's speed. Crucially, so would anyone else watching from outside the plane – even if they were standing still as it flew past.

Rather than space and time being the fixed stage, Einstein's model chose the speed of light as the one constant in our universe. His subsequent calculations led to some outcomes that make the crazy world of quantum mechanics look almost normal. Let us try to figure out why.

Imagine that our scientist on board the flying plane shines a torch at a mirror in front of her. The light will reflect straight back to her. Our observer on the ground is also able to see this happen. According to Einstein, both must agree on the speed of the beam.

For our scientist, this beam has simply travelled to the mirror and back. For the other observer, looking up and watching the scientist from the ground, however, the beam has done that and also moved along with the plane. Agreeing on speed but not agreeing on distance covered has a brain-bending outcome: the two will disagree on the *time taken*. Both have watched the same event, but for the ground-based observer, it has taken longer. As a result, he is forced into forming an unsettling conclusion: time must be running more slowly on the plane.

At first, this sounds patently ridiculous. How can time slow down at all, let alone slow down for one person and not another? Yet Einstein's theory does not stop there. The same core principles tell us that the plane and scientist will *change shape* – a consequence of the fact that Einstein's equations get rid of absolute space, too. Before we throw our hands up and declare the whole thing to be clearly madness, though, we should remember the lessons from Chapter 4.

Sometimes ideas – even intuitive ones that are held very deeply – can be wrong, and we must be prepared, always, to change our minds. Einstein's ideas above can be tested experimentally, and they have been. Amazingly, a clock on a fast-flying plane really does run more slowly than an identical one on the ground. This is not a problem with the clock; time on the plane slows down by precisely the amount Einstein predicted it would. His work is supported by evidence.

This was supposed to be a story of pain and of hope, but we are yet to touch on either. So far, it is a tale of unmitigated success, and there is no sign of the scientific heartache (or hope of resolution) that was to result from Einstein's work. We must continue with him for a little longer. Staggeringly, he was not yet finished. Having shown that Newton's supposedly rigid space and time framework could be squashed and stretched, Einstein would next demonstrate that it could also be bent – but he would need the help of Newton to do so.

Introducing Gravity

There was still a significant gap in Einstein's model, and we can find it by thinking once again about our scientist on the blacked-out plane. Let us imagine that she is asked a slightly different question: is the plane sitting still on the runway, or is it accelerating towards take-off?

This time, she *can* tell the difference. If the plane is getting faster, she will most certainly know about it, since she will be pushed backwards into her seat. This is because *acceleration* changes the game.

Performing Newtonian experiments on an accelerating plane gives noticeably different results. Balls will not fall vertically downwards any more; they will follow a curved path. They will not sit at rest on the floor any more; they will roll. Our scientist knows whether she is accelerating or not; she can *feel* it.

Einstein wasn't satisfied with this. He wanted his invariance to include acceleration; but if acceleration makes things feel different, how could this ever be done? In a moment of astonishing insight,

Einstein realized that acceleration was not perhaps as distinctive as everyone had thought. To try and understand how he did so, we will need to have in mind a bizarre mental picture: that of our plane (with scientist still on board) standing stock-still on the runway, but facing *upwards*, balancing (somehow) on its tail, with its nose pointing vertically upwards into the sky.

What will be the experience of our experimenter? As the plane stands there facing the heavens, she will feel herself being pushed into the back of her seat. This is just like her earlier experience, accelerating down the runway, but now she is *stationary*. It is no longer the acceleration of the plane that is forcing her back against the chair. It is *gravity*.

Einstein had made another key breakthrough. He declared that no one could tell the difference between feeling acceleration and feeling gravity; they could never know which one of the two was responsible for the physics around them.

When a lift begins to accelerate upwards, for example, we feel a small additional force downwards. Einstein pointed out that we would feel exactly the same thing in a stationary lift if the Earth's gravity were suddenly to increase slightly. There would be no way of telling which had really happened, because gravity and acceleration feel identical.

Einstein's invariance system of general relativity was now complete. His ingenious analysis allowed any scientists undergoing acceleration to pretend that they weren't. Instead, they could think of themselves as being stationary – and, therefore, use Newton's laws – by writing off their acceleration as an easily calculable change in gravity.

There is a wonderful symmetry to it all: Einstein had taken the jewel of Newton's crown – gravitational theory – and used it to build a brand new fixed stage for physics. What he did not know at the time, though, was that the geometrical side-effects of all this would eventually rip the entire discipline in two.

Curved Straight Lines

Once the link between acceleration and gravity was in place, the finishing line was in sight. Einstein had already destroyed the absoluteness of space and time. The squashing of lengths and slowing of durations for objects in motion was firmly established. Time and space were not rigid at all; they changed shape with speed and acceleration.

in a final flourish, however, Einstein would take on that legend of mathematical shape himself: Euclid. We have already encountered Euclid's geometry in Chapter 3. Built on his five axioms, it formed a complete system with fixed rules – such as the angles inside a triangle totalling 180°. Well-behaved and elegant, Euclid's shape-world still rules the roost in pre-university maths. General relativity, however, protested. It wasn't going to play by his rules.

When Einstein included the effects of squashed space and time on his accelerating objects, a different, "non-Euclidean" geometry appeared. Angles inside triangles could add up to just about anything. Riemann (Chapter 3) had already toyed around with imaginary worlds like this, but Einstein was not playing games; his theory described our reality. Whatever this new, crazy geometry was, it wasn't going away: it was real.

The space–time grid that underpins our whole existence was clearly fundamentally different to the neat diagrams and theorems found in school textbooks. Yet how can it be that real space–time triangles don't behave like Euclid's? The answer can be found in an old riddle:

A bear walks 5 miles south; then 5 miles west; then 5 miles north.
It is now back at its starting point. What colour is the bear?

The answer – as many will already know – is "white". Let us consider why.

At the heart of the puzzle is the fact that the three-legged journey must, somehow, be a triangle, because the bear ends up at its origin. This seems impossible at first, since the animal makes two 90° turns, which would usually map out the edges of a square. So which is it? What on earth is going on?

If the bear begins at the North Pole, however, the contradiction disappears, as we shall soon see. It is, therefore, a polar bear, hence the answer "white". (Some people then complain that polar bears are not *really* white – but that is the colour they appear to be to our eyes, even if their hairs are actually clear and hollow.) Why, though, is the North Pole so significant to this puzzle?

It is a matter of geometry. By starting there, our bear can both walk a triangular path and turn through 90° each time. Picturing the animal's journey on a globe quickly makes this clear. It walks south, then west, then north, forming a nice neat closed three-sided shape. But this is no ordinary triangle: its internal angles add up to more than 180°.

This does not mean that we have to throw the solution out as wrong. Instead, it tells us that we are deep within non-Euclidean geometry and, as we saw in Chapter 3, that only happens when the surface our shape is drawn on is *curved*. The bear's path forms a bendy, warped triangle laid down over the curved surface of a sphere; but it is a triangle nonetheless.

Einstein's new sums revealed that as objects accelerated, the same effect kicked in – their geometry became non-Euclidean. There is only one way that this could possibly make sense: the universe that these objects were moving in must have folded and twisted too. The act of accelerating actually bent space.

One final and dramatic conclusion remains. If acceleration causes space–time to warp in this way, it has a profound implication. Einstein's theory stated that acceleration and gravity were completely indistinguishable: anything acceleration does, gravity does. If general relativity really does describe our universe, we are left with a jaw-dropping result: *gravity bends space*. It is a beautiful and astonishing discovery. Newton may have produced a usable set of instructions for gravity, but he had never been able to explain how it *worked*. He told his friend, the scholar Richard Bentley (1662–1742), that he saw it as a challenge for those studying his text:

> Gravity must be caused by an agent acting constantly according to certain laws, but whether this agent be material or immaterial, I have left to the consideration of my readers.[4]

Now, 230 years later, a "reader" had cracked it. Einstein had an explanation for gravity. According to general relativity, any mass would cause the space–time around it to bend: more mass, more curvature. A huge mass like the Sun warped space so much that the planets orbiting it were simply following the bent space around it. In fact, as far as they were concerned, the planets were effectively moving along straight lines on the grid – blissfully unaware that the grid itself had changed shape – curved by the Sun's gravity.

General relativity came with a built-in test of authenticity: it predicted that light would also follow the grid's "curved straight lines". This was checkable: did the presence of the Sun "bend" light from the stars behind it as it moved across the sky? In 1919, the great English physicist Sir Arthur Eddington (1882–1944) took advantage of a total eclipse to find out. His conclusion was emphatic: general relativity was correct.[5]

Einstein's curved-space-and-time theory is mad, beautiful, and accurate. It is one of the great triumphs in human thought. It tells us something deep about the universe we live in, something both surprising and captivating. That, in itself, would be enough reason to tell its story, even without considering the subject of this chapter. The theme we began it with, however, has still not emerged from this odd geometrical tale. What does general relativity have to do with scientific *suffering*? What does it have to do with scientific *hope*?

Trouble

A book entitled *The Trouble with Physics* could easily bring to mind some of Chapter 1's more negative views of science. Does it echo Keats's concerns about physics ruining our sense of wonder? Is it a pessimistic or cynical criticism of the money-driven technology industry? Has a priest written a fiery religious work declaring science to be godless? In reality, none of these apply. The author, Lee Smolin, is a theoretical physicist – a rather frustrated one, in fact.[6] For physics, as the title of the book suggests, really has got itself into quite a bit of trouble.

The issue at hand manages to be both wonderfully simple and mind-bogglingly complex, and it involves two of the powerhouse theories of twentieth-century physics: quantum mechanics and general relativity. General relativity describes the universe on its largest scales with pinpoint accuracy; quantum mechanics deals with the microscopic without missing a beat. Between them, therefore, they cover the whole realm of physical reality. So what's the issue?

To say that entire books have been written on this question is an understatement. A brief survey of available material will show that entire books have been written just about the books that have been written on this question. It is perhaps surprising, then, that the cause of the upset is actually quite simple to state: general relativity and quantum mechanics are in disagreement. If one theory is correct, then no matter how accurate or beautiful or rigorous the other might be, it is wrong.

Tied up within the mathematics of general relativity is the statement that space is *smooth*. Yes, it can be squashed, twisted, warped, and folded, but it remains a smooth, unpunctured surface nonetheless. The equations of quantum mechanics, however, paint a different picture: space is full of holes. It froths around violently, riddled with gaps and cavities and foaminess. The truth is unavoidable: until this contradiction is remedied, physics is broken.

Following GUT Feelings

Einstein was on to this. He knew that his relativistic description of gravity didn't *fit*. It became a mission of his to find a home for it with quantum mechanics. This is entirely understandable: science is the pursuit of deep wisdom about nature, and what could be deeper than a model that would describe *all* of it? This is the search for what some call the Grand Unified Theory (GUT), and it is the ultimate goal of theoretical physicists everywhere. The concept of a GUT appears to have broken through into the mainstream – so much so, that even Hollywood A-lister Will Smith surprised *New York* magazine with this revelation:

> I'm a student of patterns. At heart, I'm a physicist. I look at everything in my life as trying to find the single equation, the Theory of Everything.[7]

Nearly a century after Einstein began his attempts to find exactly this equation, the hunt continues. It is a journey of both hope and pain. There is hope that an answer exists and there is pain because it has not yet appeared. Sometimes the task is lonely and thankless, as theoretician Brian Greene observes:

> For long stretches during those decades [Einstein] was the sole searcher for such a unified theory, and his passionate yet solitary quest alienated him from the mainstream physics community.[8]

Einstein never got his answer. Just as Robert Brown died before unlocking the mystery of his "ever-present motion" and Ignaz Semmelweis was killed before the discovery of germs, the mighty German left this life without a solution. In their scientific work all three of them suffered, intellectually at the very least. What kept them going was hope – and this hope did not die when they did.

An Answer with Strings Attached

Brian Greene has brought far more to science than just biographies of great physicists; he is one of the cheerleaders for a GUT candidate known often as "string theory". String theory is an attempt to bring quantum mechanics and general relativity together in wonderful non-contradictory harmony.

Like the two warring worldviews, it is predominantly mathematical – more so, even. In essence, string theory limits how closely we can "zoom in" on space when we look at it. It therefore prevents us from saying whether space is smooth or whether it has holes, because we can't see the surface well enough to be sure. The contradiction literally disappears from view.

For those who think this is a correct way of heading towards our GUT, the final equation is within reach: it will be found within string theory once it is fully understood. For those who do not think it is correct, string theory is simply mathematical cheating with no grounding in the physical world. Neither group is shy in putting its point across. First, here is Greene:

> String theory is the most developed theory with the capacity to unite general relativity and quantum mechanics in a consistent manner. I do believe the universe is consistent, and therefore I do believe that general relativity and quantum mechanics should be put together in a manner that makes sense.[9]

And, countering with the accusation that this is all self-deception at best and dishonesty at worst, here is Smolin, raging at the vast number of variations and of unknowns in the string theory world:

> We understand very little about most of these string theories. And of the small number we understand in any detail, every single one disagrees with the present experimental data, usually in at least two ways.[10]

The slanging match has continued ever since, with not much being held back. Smolin's book has been described as "irrational" and "anti-scientific" by Lubos Motl,[11] while string theory is labelled "unattractive" and as having "no evidence whatsoever" by Peter Woit.[12] Both men are accomplished physicists and university lecturers who have popular blogs. The ongoing battle between the two sides even has a name: the "string wars".[13]

So where does this leave us? To date, a century after Einstein tried to get everything to fit, we still have no answer. Feelings are running high. Many string theorists may have to face up to the reality that they will go the same way as Brown, Semmelweis, and Einstein: answerless.

Yet this is the risk all scientists run; there is no realistic alternative. Stuck in their own "Steiner Saturdays", they are pushed ever onwards by those twin impressions that constantly nag at humanity: that "things aren't right" and that "there is better to come". Without these two convictions, science would be brought to its knees. Where, then, do they – and the accompanying responses of pain and hope – come from?

Paradise Lost and Found?

There are many creation texts of many different genres within the Bible, but one is by far the best known – that of Adam, Eve, and the garden of Eden. The first two human beings are portrayed as being part of a flawless natural world and as enjoying a loving and fulfilling relationship with their creator God.

Then, in a series of events that has become known in Christian theology as "the Fall", the book of Genesis describes Adam and Eve's rejection of God's authority, wisdom, and love, urged on by an evil character called the "serpent". They are dismissed from the garden and God pronounces a further punishment:

> Cursed is the ground because of you;
> through painful toil you will eat food from it all the days of your life
> It will produce thorns and thistles for you.[14]

Previously, Adam and Eve had lived in peace with nature; now their coexistence would be a struggle. The relationship between humans and the creation around them was now damaged. As a result, theirs would be a fight to understand it, a fight to benefit from it and a fight to enjoy it.

Wisdom about nature would have to be hard won: it would be *painful toil*. In this same passage, though, God ensures that Adam and Eve are not left without hope. He hints that, one day, a decisive victory for humankind will be won over evil. God declares to the serpent:

> I will put enmity
> between you and the woman,
> and between your offspring and hers;
> he will crush your head.[15]

The message of pain and hope is written all the way through Scripture, from beginning to end. In many cases, these passages refer to nature.

Once again, we can find our theme in Job:

> Do not mortals have hard service on earth?
> Are not their days like those of hired labourers?
> Like a slave longing for the evening shadows,
> or a hired labourer waiting to be paid,
> so I have been allotted months of futility,
> and nights of misery have been assigned to me.[16]

Job laments his suffering, and does not consider it unique to himself: all *mortals* are in the same position. Life here is *hard service*. And yet, despite this struggle, he holds firmly to the conviction that there will be resolution brought about, somehow, in the future:

> I know that my Redeemer lives,
> and that in the end he will stand on the earth.
> And after my skin has been destroyed,
> yet in my flesh I will see God;
> I myself will see him
> with my own eyes — I, and not another.
> How my heart yearns within me![17]

Job's view that things should – and will eventually – be different is shared by three of his friends, seeking to act as both counsellors and comforters. Although much of what they say is not helpful or insightful, we can still see evidence of the human hope for a better relationship with nature. It is suggested to Job that, if he learns from God and lives a holier life:

> You will be protected from the lash of the tongue,
> and need not fear when destruction comes.
> You will laugh at destruction and famine,
> and need not fear the wild animals.
> For you will have a covenant with the stones of the field,
> and the wild animals will be at peace with you.[18]

The notion of a *covenant with the stones* here summons up a world in which humanity and creation are operating with a togetherness that really works. For "covenant", read "relationship". It speaks of an ideal that was first founded in Eden before the Fall and that could be brought back again.

In fact, biblical pictures of this restoration to come are always focused on relationships: God with humankind, humankind with nature, and even nature with itself. Through the prophet Isaiah, God himself says:

> "For as the days of a tree,
> so will be the days of my people;
> my chosen ones will long enjoy
> the work of their hands.
> They will not labour in vain,
> nor will they bear children doomed to misfortune;
> for they will be a people blessed by the Lord,
> they and their descendants with them.
> Before they call I will answer;
> while they are still speaking I will hear.
> The wolf and the lamb will feed together,
> and the lion will eat straw like the ox…
> They will neither harm nor destroy
> on all my holy mountain," says the Lord.[19]

Genesis, Isaiah, and Job are all Old Testament books, but we find the same trumpet call in the New Testament too. It also tells us that life is hard, but that there is hope.

Groaning Creations, New Creations

Just as Job provides us with a steady source of insight in the Old Testament, the apostle Paul illuminates our way in the New. We already know that Job suffered horrifically; so did Paul. He was beaten, stoned, shipwrecked, flogged, and left for dead. On top of this, he was continually insulted, defamed, and subjected to unjust trials.

All of this came as a direct result of his dramatic about-face on the Damascus road. Paul was preaching and teaching that Jesus was God, and he was often attacked violently for doing so. Why keep going along a path that brought so much pain? In laying out his reasons for carrying on with his calling, he draws parallels with the suffering-and-hope story of nature itself:

> I consider that our present sufferings are not worth comparing
> with the glory that will be revealed in us. For the creation waits in
> eager expectation for the children of God to be revealed. For the
> creation was subjected to frustration, not by its own choice, but

by the will of the one who subjected it, in hope that the creation itself will be liberated from its bondage to decay and brought into the freedom and glory of the children of God.

We know that the whole creation has been groaning as in the pains of childbirth right up to the present time. Not only so, but we ourselves, who have the firstfruits of the Spirit, groan inwardly as we wait eagerly for our adoption to sonship, the redemption of our bodies. For in this hope we were saved.[20]

Paul sees his own personal story and that of creation as interlinked. He is suffering and so is the Earth. He is longing for better and the physical world is too. His body will be redeemed and creation will be liberated. It is this hope of a restored God–humanity–universe relationship that keeps him pressing on.

Again and again, the Bible claims that both nature and humanity are not as they really should be; they are not as they were when first created. Again and again, stories are told of a full restoration. In the last book of the Bible, Revelation, the Fall is undone and a brand new creation is revealed, mirroring Eden. It is a place of perfection in which God and humanity live together:

Then the angel showed me the river of the water of life, as clear as crystal, flowing from the throne of God and of the Lamb down the middle of the great street of the city. On each side of the river stood the tree of life, bearing twelve crops of fruit, yielding its fruit every month. And the leaves of the tree are for the healing of the nations. No longer will there be any curse.[21]

Thus, from beginning to end, the Bible is a story of potential, loss, pain, and hope. So often, science echoes these during the search for understanding. A glimpse is caught of a profound truth. Confusion and failure set in, sometimes for lifetimes, before – wonderfully – nature gives up its answers, with hints of yet more to come.

For Brown, Semmelweis, and Einstein, as for so many others, theirs was a science-life lived within the frustration and hurt of a battle. Does the Bible have anything to say to today's scientists who may be experiencing the same?

Take Heart!

Christians live life in tension. First, they have a conviction that the world and humanity have fallen. Relationships of all kinds are damaged, limited, and strained. The human race is in at least partial ignorance of nature, just as they are in at least partial ignorance of their Maker. The "covenant with the stones" has gone the same way as the covenant with God.

Second, however, they have promises from Scripture which give them a much more positive view of what is yet to come, and they look forward to a day in which all is resolved. The Bible is, therefore, both realistic and hopeful. So what should the Christian do in the meantime? The answer is found throughout the New Testament: seek to bring as much of the longed-for future good as is possible into the present.

Far from simply sitting on their hands, waiting for Jesus to come back and fix everything, the apostle Peter urges the first Christians to bring about restoration in their own sphere in any way that they feasibly can. Directly linking hope about the future with committed effort in the day-to-day, he says:

> [God] has given us his very great and precious promises... For this very reason, make every effort to add to your faith goodness; and to goodness, knowledge; and to knowledge, self-control; and to self-control, perseverance; and to perseverance, godliness; and to godliness, mutual affection; and to mutual affection, love. For if you possess these qualities in increasing measure, they will keep you from being ineffective and unproductive... you will receive a rich welcome into the eternal kingdom of our Lord and Saviour Jesus Christ.[22]

It is precisely the belief that things will come good at some further-off point in the future that motivates the Christian to work for that same goodness right now. As Jesus himself declared earlier to the disciples (including Peter): "In this world, you will have trouble. But take heart! I have overcome the world."[23]

Can this mentality help in the laboratory? We have learned in this chapter that science is often confusing, painful, frustrating, and incomplete. A scientist can spend their life seeking to solve a problem and fail. Sometimes this has huge ramifications on the lives of others, as with Semmelweis; sometimes the suffering is only intellectual and personal, as with Brown. How can an individual keep pursuing wisdom about nature when it is difficult or disheartening? Where will that perseverance come from?

The parallel between the biblical big picture and real scientific experience is striking. The Bible teaches of a future moral perfection and uses this hope as a powerful motivation to bring forth moral improvement today, even when the process is hard work. It also teaches that we will one day have a full and functional scientific understanding of creation – a *covenant with the stones* – and so the conclusion must be the same.

Scientists, therefore, are to work hard – even in great adversity – to seek out this understanding now. Just as moral breakthroughs can bring joy and rejoicing in the present, scientific breakthroughs can too. Both can also serve to remind us that we are looking forward to something even better.

The struggling researcher would do well to remember those words of Jesus. Yes, things aren't right. Yes, they should be better. And yes, in this scientific world, there will be trouble. But in the fight to bring distant restoration nearer, scientists are God-approved workers.

What better preparation could there be for difficult days with magnets, microscopes, or mass spectrometers? As they walk into the lab, unsure of how things will go, Jesus says they can have hope. He says they can *take heart*.

6

ORDER FROM CHAOS

I am God, and there is none like Me, declaring the end
from the beginning.

God, in Isaiah (KJV)

I never predict anything, and I never will.

Paul Gascoigne

The British playwright Sir Tom Stoppard has an impressive back
catalogue of stage and cinema hits to his name. Of these, the one
with the highest profile among the general public is probably the
1998 romance *Shakespeare in Love*, which he co-wrote. Another of his
works, however, is more deeply loved and appreciated by those in the
know – a play that has proved to be hugely influential in the world
of art and entertainment ever since its first performance in 1966. Its
mouthful of a title is *Rosencrantz and Guildenstern are Dead*.[1]

Rosencrantz and Guildenstern are minor characters in Shakespeare's
Hamlet. Stoppard turns the tables: he brings the duo centre stage and
tells *their* story, relegating the original's main players to the wings. In
doing so, he was years ahead of his time; the concept of "reimagining"
an existing story is now commonplace and has spawned countless
films and books in the last few decades.

Stoppard's groundbreaking script toys with the fact that the
centuries-old plot has *already been written*: the two men have a fixed,
inescapable future. This idea is introduced to both the audience
and the central pairing right at the very start of the tale: Stoppard
opens with Rosencrantz and Guildenstern playing a simple game of
chance. It becomes clear, fairly quickly, that something is not quite
right.

Guildenstern takes a coin from his bag, flips it, and then announces
the result. If it is heads, it goes to Rosencrantz. Presumably, if it is
tails, he keeps it – but we never find out. This is because, for each

successive coin toss, the outcome is the same – heads every time – and yet neither man is cheating, and the coins are fair.

As their conversation goes on, we find out that this game has been under way for quite some time, with Rosencrantz steadily getting richer and richer. He does not react to this with any sense of surprise, but Guildenstern becomes increasingly uneasy about the whole thing:

> A weaker man might be moved to re-examine his faith, if in
> nothing else at least in the law of probability.

He seeks to reason his way through possible causes. Might he be secretly desiring the loss and somehow making it happen? Might they be stuck in a time-loop, witnessing the same coin toss again and again? Could it simply be proof that each toss is a brand new event, not dependent on any previous result? Most outlandish of all: are they being subjected to unnatural forces of some kind?

As Guildenstern becomes more and more panicked by the situation, he appeals to *science* to calm his nerves, suggesting that he and his colleague discuss the run of heads rationally:

> A scientific approach to the examination of phenomena is a
> defence against the pure emotion of fear.

Over the next few exchanges, the audience learns about events that occurred prior to the start of the play. It is revealed that the game had not always been going this way. In fact, it had been roughly even until the pair were given a message by a courier. Only since the courier's visit have the coins shown this unsettling one-sided behaviour.

During his musings on all this, Guildenstern makes a point that will be of great importance to us as this chapter develops. He considers the earlier, random coin tosses that levelled out the two men's finances and declares:

> This made for a kind of harmony and a kind of confidence. It
> related the fortuitous and the ordained into a reassuring union
> which we recognised as nature. The sun came up about as often
> as it went down, in the long run, and a coin showed heads about
> as often as it showed tails. Then a messenger arrived. We had
> been sent for. Nothing else happened. Ninety-two coins spun
> consecutively have come down heads ninety-two consecutive
> times...

Something deep within Guildenstern – and us – says that ninety-two heads in a row should not happen. It just doesn't fit with what we would *predict*.

On the other hand, it is generally agreed that coin flips are decided by *chance*. Somehow, then, we see the outcome as both random *and* predictable. How can this be? Are we being irrational, or is there something deeper going on? Is Guildenstern right when he says this strange idea of "predictable randomness" brings *harmony* and *confidence*? To find an answer, we will follow his recommendation – and take a *scientific approach*.

Figuring Everything Out

Perhaps we should first take one step back and ask whether coin tosses actually *are* random. Some would claim that the answer is a rather obvious "yes". If they weren't, then they would not be considered a "fair" method of deciding an outcome.

Over much of football's history, for instance, drawn matches that could not be replayed went to a coin toss. In 1968, Italy progressed to the final of the European Championships when their captain correctly called tails, with Russia being the unlucky losers. If heads and tails were not considered equally likely, no one would go along with this practice.

Italy, as it happens, went on to win the tournament. Two years later, the dreaded penalty shootout was introduced, as an attempt to put teams through on sporting merit rather than pure chance. But is a coin toss really a thing of chance?

Three mathematicians – Persi Diaconis, Susan Holmes, and Richard Montgomery – have studied this issue in some depth.[2] In their analysis, they considered how the problem could be tackled with some sort of mathematical structure in place. They zeroed-in on two pieces of information: how fast the coin was spinning and how fast it initially moved upwards. Having crunched the data and then compared it with real-life physiology, they had their answer:

For natural flips, the chance of coming up as started is about .51

In other words, a coin showing heads and then tossed in the air by the average human being will come down showing heads 51 times out of 100. At first, this would appear to be potentially useful information, but does it actually answer our question? Does it tell us whether or not coin tosses are random?

The reason that this work is of some help to us is not so much its final conclusion, but in the process of getting to it. It seems that the more physical information we know about the beginning of the flip, the more we can know about its result. What would happen, then, if we were to know *every* piece of physical information at the start?

If we knew the number and type of particles in the coin, the exact force applied to it, the temperature of the room, the strength of any breeze, and so on, would we then be able to describe the outcome with certainty? If so, could this idea be extended to other, more complex events? If we had enough data, might we be able to predict *everything*?

These questions are not new. Once Newton developed his laws of motion, the basis was there for the discussion: could we, somehow, use these laws to calculate the future perfectly? The French mathematician Pierre-Simon Laplace (1749–1827) is perhaps most responsible for popularizing the concept:

> An intellect which at a certain moment would know all forces that set nature in motion, and all positions of all items of which nature is composed, if this intellect were also vast enough to submit these data to analysis, it would embrace in a single formula the movements of the greatest bodies of the universe and those of the tiniest atom; for such an intellect nothing would be uncertain and the future just like the past would be present before its eyes.[3]

Laplace is claiming that a mechanical universe following fixed laws is completely predictable if both the laws and the current measurements for every part of it are known. In this model, the universe is essentially a machine; raw data and maths are all that are needed to know everything yet to come. The future is fixed because it depends only on what is where in the present. This view of our world is known as "determinism".

In determinism, it is not just the result of a coin toss that can be calculated. Nothing is out of reach. Provided there is enough data on board, the determinist can state in advance all the events, deeds, and even thoughts associated with humanity – or other life forms – in fine detail.

Heads versus tails seems like a small issue in comparison to this. Is it feasible, though? What does modern science have to say about determinism? Is this locked-in, machine-like universe of Laplace the one that scientists actually find themselves working in? Is our world – are we – predictable, or random?

How Wrong is Wrong?

Seeking to apply Laplace's ideas in the real world means following two separate processes. Any potential *intellect* must first gather *all positions of all items* and then second *submit these data to analysis*. The second phase requires the correct laws to be used, of course – but then humanity is pretty good at discovering those, as we have seen. It is actually the first step – gathering the data – that proves to be the tricky one.

Collecting data means taking measurements, and taking measurements means using some sort of equipment. In the last few centuries, significant technological advances have been made in many different fields – notably electromagnetism and quantum mechanics – and our measuring devices have thus become more and more powerful.

There exist, for example, light detectors that can pick up a single photon. There are scales that can weigh a single hydrogen atom.[4] There are even magnetometers that can sense the magnetic effects of the Earth on a single red blood cell.[5] It is therefore currently possible to obtain results from all sorts of experiments to almost unimaginable detail. Is "almost unimaginable detail" actually good enough, though?

What happens if we use these very-good-but-not-quite-perfect readings in our calculations? Do they give results which agree with those observed in real life? In many cases, yes. The fact that our measurements are not exact does not end up having any major effect. The tiny, unknown inaccuracies in the starting data either disappear or stay very small. As a result, a well-behaved solution emerges.

One famous example of this is the "simple pendulum" – picture a mass on the end of string, swinging back and forth. We might not know the precise value for the initial speed of the swing or for the pull of gravity on the mass, but when our calculations predict regular, steady motion, they are found to be correct. Laplace would be happy: here, we really are able to predict the future.

There are other systems, however, where being even slightly wrong at the beginning really does make a huge difference. One of the most famous examples is found in the work of the remarkable biologist Baron Robert May of Oxford. Once President of the Royal Society, May has also worked as the Chief Science Adviser to the UK government. And, in a 1976 paper entitled "Simple Mathematical Models with Very Complicated Dynamics", he drew the scientific world's attention to something more than just a little strange.[6]

May had been attempting to model changes in animal populations over time, and his process was very straightforward. He would enter a starting population into a single short equation, which would spit out a new number. This value was then put into the same equation again to get the next one, and so on. The resulting sequence represented the animal population year-on-year. The equation May used was not a complicated one; his work could be carried out with relative ease by anyone armed with a pocket calculator.

As might be expected from a simple question, May initially found simple answers. His equation included a number for the growth-rate of the population (labelled r), a number that could be adjusted by the user. When r was set fairly low, the model either settled down on a fixed, steady population (150, 150, 150, 150...) or predicted a repetitive high–low–high–low (150, 80, 150, 80...) year-on-year. In other words, low-r predictions were always nice and tidy patterns.

These low-r solutions had the added bonus of behaving in the same way as the pendulum: if the starting population was altered a little bit, it didn't matter. This small "error" would soon disappear and the prediction would end up being the same as it was for the unaltered value. Being a little bit "wrong" at the start was OK; the maths sorted itself out.

Hidden deep inside May's model, however, was a surprise. When r was increased above a certain value, the predictions suddenly took on a new "random" appearance. The equation and the method were the same as before, but now populations could be high for years in a row, then hover around the middle, then collapse, then see a period of flipping between high and low. It appeared that, within results like these (134, 125, 22, 90...) there was no pattern to be seen whatsoever.

It is worth noting that a lack of a pattern does not necessarily mean that a sequence is random. Testing for real randomness is more complex than that, but a useful first step is (thankfully) a simple one: run the calculations again from the start. In cases of real randomness, an entirely new set of results will emerge each time.

When May re-ran his higher-r sums, however, he kept producing exactly the same sequence. The population prediction might well have looked random, but it wasn't. Despite its odd appearance, it was a repeatable, fixed-future solution. And, as May was about to discover, it had yet another trick up its sleeve.

This time, changing the first-year population by even the tiniest of amounts made a dramatic difference to the resulting sequence. Amazingly, an inaccuracy as small as just one animal in a billion would lead to a totally new patternless prediction, unrecognizable when compared to the first. The two predictions could differ by millions of animals after just a few years. Rather than disappearing over time, the most modest of errors at the beginning led to a drastically altered future.

This type of behaviour – in which the results produced are so utterly dependent on the very first piece of data entered – is now known as "chaotic". Animal populations are by no means the only chaotic systems. They have been discovered, in fact, in just about every field of science that can be imagined.

In the most famous example, Edward Lorenz (1917–2008) demonstrated – accidentally – that some mathematical models of weather are chaotic too. In 1961, he was using a computer which worked to six decimal places. Lorenz wanted to run a simulation a second time, but re-entered the data with only three decimal places, thinking it wouldn't matter. The tiny difference (one part in 10,000) between the number Lorenz entered and the one his computer had used previously gave two radically different weather predictions.[7]

Lorenz famously described his findings as the "butterfly effect". His claim was that an effect as small as an insect's wingbeat is enough to alter predictions from breezes to tornados. A slightly longer – and less attractive – name for the butterfly effect is "sensitive dependence upon initial conditions".

It is not unreasonable to say that chaotic systems are therefore both predictable *and* random. If we had access to perfect starting data, we would be able to say with absolute certainty what will happen, because the equations are known. Running the process again gives the same results every time, so the future is guaranteed.

In practice, though, we are stuck. Our real-world measurements will always have errors because we will never have perfect equipment. What May and Lorenz have shown is that even the smallest of these errors is enough to change the whole game – so the future becomes a matter of chance.

As a result, chaos theory tells us that there really is underlying structure and order in this world, but that we will never be able to fully access it. Animal populations and weather patterns are indeed under tight mathematical control, but we can't ever know what they will do more than a few steps down the line. Lorenz himself puts it very well: "The present determines the future, but the approximate present does not approximately determine the future."[8]

In chaos, then, the "randomness" is entirely caused by our errors. Guildenstern and Rosencrantz's coin flips are not *truly* random: the outcome could, theoretically, be calculated every time. In reality, though, they may as well be, for the two men can never start with perfect data.

Would Guildenstern thank us for this? Would he be reassured that all is well? Presumably not – ninety-two consecutive heads still feels wrong, even after our discussion of chaos. Let us push the investigation further: does "real" randomness ever exist? We didn't find it in coin tosses, animal populations or weather, but can we find it elsewhere in science?

Seeing the Bigger Picture

Liquids, on any real-world scale, consist of overwhelmingly large numbers of particles. We know from earlier chapters that these involve themselves in non-stop frantic jiggling; Brown saw the effects of this at the larger scale, and Einstein calculated it at the smaller. Although we know the rules that any one particle will obey as it crashes around, we find, in reality, that its behaviour is hopelessly unknowable for us. Why is this?

The answer is annoyingly simple: there are too many particles involved. Trying to keep track of all of the frantic collisions among the writhing mess of trillions of molecules is beyond any equipment we have and beyond our calculating power. This is not something that will be solved by waiting for better technology to come along: the numbers are too big, and they always will be.

What is odd about this, though, is that our complete inability to figure out what the separate particles are doing does not result in the liquid as a whole becoming a mystery. Even a young child can play with water and know what to expect. Its behaviour is predictable for us. How can this be true? How can we predict the whole if we have no idea at all what its parts are doing?

Perhaps the key breakthrough in answering this question came from a man who has already been encountered in our travels: James Clerk Maxwell. When working on ideas about gas particles spreading out as they collided with others, he called on the concept of *probability* for help.

Well aware that any attempt to calculate the individual speeds of molecules would be impossible, Maxwell's brilliant idea was to try treating them all at once. He assumed that a certain fraction of the particles would travel at one speed, another fraction at another and so on, allowing him to build up an overall picture without ever having to know what any one particle was doing.

To see why this step was a huge help, let us consider dice rolls. When rolling just one die, we cannot say what the outcome will be. This uncertainty is not a problem, though, if we increase the number of dice. When rolling six million of them, for example, we can be pretty sure that we will get about one million of each number. We still have no idea at all what any individual die will do, but we can confidently predict the overall result and, in the case of a gas or liquid, it is only the overall result that we need.

Maxwell's work was progressed significantly by Ludwig Boltzmann (1844–1906), and the new science that resulted became known as statistical mechanics. It follows the same basic principles as our dice-roll argument above: use probabilities rather than actual values and then make a prediction that says what will *probably* happen.

Provided there are enough particles (and there always are), what statistical mechanics says will probably happen turns out to be so overwhelmingly likely that it actually *does* happen – every time. In this way, we can arrive at powerful and accurate descriptions of liquid and gas behaviour. Marvellously, rather than working against us, the unknown behaviour of the individual particles actually works for us – without it, statistical mechanics wouldn't be valid. Once again, as with chaos, we find that randomness and predictability are more closely related than we might ever have thought.

Statistical mechanics deliberately treats individual particle movement as random in order to produce answers about the overall system – but the movement isn't actually random at all. The laws of physics really do describe exactly what is going on within a liquid or gas. It is only because we cannot ever manage this in practice that we revert to the probabilistic approach and "pretend" that the particles behave randomly. If Chaos isn't "real" randomness, and if statistical mechanics isn't either, is that the end of our search? Not quite.

Quantum Mechanics to the Rescue

Whenever a light particle – a photon – reaches a pane of glass, it has three possible futures. First, it could be absorbed, its energy adding to that of the glass. We shall call this possibility A. Second, it could pass straight through (P). Third, it could reflect back from the surface (R). Firing 100 identical photons at a pane, one after the other, will therefore give a sequence of results that might look like this: A, P, P, R, P, P, A, A... and so on.

Crucially, this process *does* pass our earlier test for randomness: repeat the same experiment, and a new sequence appears each time. This is because we have re-entered the crazy world of quantum mechanics – and this time the uncertainty is built in.

In chaos theory, "randomness" results from not using exact data at the start; in statistical mechanics it is deliberately introduced by us to deal with the sheer number of particles involved. In quantum mechanics, however, even perfect data used on just a single photon will not remove it. Uncertainty comes as part of the package; we can never be sure what a quantum particle will do.

Does this mean that whole systems built up of quantum parts are also unknowable? Not entirely. Just as with statistical mechanics, these systems can be dealt with by considering probabilities. The random fuzziness of the individual particles gives way to a confident statement about the overall picture. Once again, we can only ever say what will probably happen and, once again, this matches wonderfully with what actually occurs.

The probabilistic approach shows us that order really can emerge from disorder. At first, the impossibility of knowing what liquid or quantum particles will do suggests we will never be able to produce reliable predictions in these areas. Despite the randomness of these tiny brushstrokes, however, the bigger picture they are painting comes right into view. Treating the entire system at once gets us answers better than we could ever have hoped for. Each individual particle is unpredictable, yes – but the same is not true of the whole.

Everything is Under Control... Sort of

What would Laplace and Guildenstern have to say about our investigation so far? Would they be impressed or comforted or annoyed or worried? Let us summarize our findings and then apply them to the two men in turn.

Chaos theory states there are systems – like animal populations and weather – that appear to be random, but aren't. They are actually the result of well-defined mathematical equations and are theoretically predictable. Without perfect starting data, though, the predictability collapses, and our hope of ever knowing the future goes with it.

Statistical mechanics deals with systems in which the huge number of particles means they cannot each be treated individually – too many separate sums would be involved. Yet by introducing man-made randomness and imagining what the particles are probably doing, we can identify a probable future; and when we do that, we are pretty much spot on.

Quantum mechanics tells us that its particles are completely unknowable, even when on their own. Thankfully, we can still use the idea of probability to predict what many of them will do when combined, and these predictions are the most accurate in all of science.

Putting all of this together tells us that there is much tighter relationship between randomness and predictability in science than anyone might ever have thought. Theoretically predictable systems collapse into randomness. Theoretically random systems coalesce into predictability. Is the future knowable, or not? It seems that science gives a rather unscientific answer: "sort of".

We can see this by considering Laplace's Intellect. This intellect would have perfect starting data and perfect calculating power, so chaotic and multi-particle systems would present no problem to it. The real issue for the intellect is quantum mechanics. Here, the unpredictability is inherent and unavoidable. The intellect would be forced into a probabilistic approach and could only declare a *probable* future, facing a tiny chance of being wrong. Because of this, Laplace's determinism breaks down, and the universe can no longer be considered a machine. There is, it would appear, a quantum spanner in the works.

What about Guildenstern and the ninety-two heads in a row? A single coin toss is chaotic and so to us it really does become random. We could ask, then, what the chances are of ninety-two straight heads with a fair coin. The answer is – unsurprisingly – that they are very small indeed.

In fact, Guildenstern and his friend Rosencrantz would have to play their game for longer than the age of the universe before they could reasonably expect this run to occur. Clearly, the chaotic randomness that seems hardwired into our "normal" nature has broken down for these particular men. This is not lost on Guildenstern:

One, probability is a factor which operates within natural forces.
Two, probability is not operating as a factor. Three, we are now within un-, sub- or supernatural forces.[9]

He is right, of course. Natural forces are not operating properly – because they are in a play. Their futures are already written. The breakdown of chance indicates the presence of a greater mind at work: that of the author. If Guildenstern, then, can learn something deeply profound about his universe by considering randomness and predictability, can we? If so, what is it? It is time to pay another visit to Job.

Almighty Disasters

Let us remind ourselves briefly of Job's story. He is a godly man who has been subjected to great mental and physical suffering, by which God will prove to "the Accuser" that Job's faithfulness is not due to his wonderful life. Job has no idea that this is what is going on. As a result, he believes that God is failing miserably in his duty to provide true justice.

In his distress, Job is not afraid to throw accusations at God. He repeatedly states that he is innocent and that God's moral compass must somehow be broken:

> For what is our lot from God above,
> our heritage from the Almighty on high?
> Is it not ruin for the wicked,
> disaster for those who do wrong?
> Does he not see my ways
> and count my every step?
>
> If I have walked with falsehood
> or my foot has hurried after deceit –
> let God weigh me in honest scales
> and he will know that I am blameless –
> if my steps have turned from the path,
> if my heart has been led by my eyes,
> or if my hands have been defiled,
> then may others eat what I have sown,
> and may my crops be uprooted.[10]

There are three points of great importance here. First, Job still believes that God is *on high*, that God can see all and is in control of the universe. Second, Job states that divine justice is supposed to result in blessings for the holy and *ruin for the wicked*. Third, he expects those blessings and ruin to be both manifest in this life and evidenced in physical creation: *uprooted crops*.

Job believes that God is *Almighty* – that he is comprehensively in charge of nature. He also believes God is making serious moral mistakes. Linking these two ideas together, Job sees a way to build his case. He will try to show that God is making a complete mess of overseeing nature. If he can do that, he thinks, God will have to admit that he is morally mistaken, too.

This is a task that Job takes on with gusto. Identifying areas within God's creation that appear to indicate divine carelessness is something that he finds rather straightforward. Again and again, Job cries out:

> He holds back the waters; there is drought;
> he lets them loose, they overwhelm the Earth.[11]

> He moves mountains without their knowing it
> and overturns them in his anger.
> He shakes the earth from its place
> and makes its pillars tremble.[12]

> As a mountain slips away and erodes,
> and a cliff is dislodged from its place;
> as water wears away stone
> and torrents scour the soil from the land –
> so you destroy man's hope.[13]

Job is becoming more and more anguished. Nature, as he points out repeatedly, is brutal at times – and it is happening on God's watch. Having referenced droughts, floods, earthquakes, and landslides, Job applies what might seem the killer blow, linking harsh nature directly with divine cruelty:

> Even if I summoned him and he responded,
> I do not believe he would give me a hearing.
> He would crush me with a storm
> and multiply my wounds for no reason.[14]

Job's case is complete. He has been wronged by a God who cannot run nature properly. The random destruction caused by natural disasters of all kinds is mirrored by the random destruction of Job as a human being. Whilst we can be pretty sure that Job didn't listen to many 1970s Dutch soft rock ballads, Margriet Eshiujs might have made his playlist if he had one. She decries God for breaking promises, failing to pay appropriate attention, ignoring prayer and starving his people. The title of this work? *God is Asleep.*

Elsewhere, though, the Bible disputes this accusation categorically. Psalms tells us that God never drifts off; in fact, he maintains a caring watch over his creation:

> He who watches over you will not slumber;
> indeed, he who watches over Israel
> will neither slumber nor sleep.[15]

And – as we are about to see – during Job's cry of foul play, God had been very much awake.

Whose Earth is it Anyway?

In a development that is both surprising and entirely fitting, God does indeed respond to Job, speaking to him and his four counsellors from within a *storm*. This is our first clue that there may be far more to the apparent randomness of nature than Job had brought to his argument. God's opening salvo makes a few things clear from the outset:

> Who is this that obscures my plans
> with words without knowledge?
> Brace yourself like a man;
> I will question you,
> and you shall answer me.[16]

These short lines are packed full of significance for us. First, God counters Job's idea of cruel chance in creation by announcing that he has *plans*. These plans would be perhaps more obvious to Job, God says, if only he had more *knowledge*. Job should now prepare himself for questioning. Unexpectedly, though, it will be not be the crushing blow that Job had earlier predicted.

Brace yourself is a translation of a phrase that was used in legal proceedings between equal parties. Job is not being required to sit in silence, but to come up with answers. As we saw in Chapter 3, Job is being invited into a new way of thinking. God will push him to examine things afresh. Could it be that randomness and overall divine care can walk hand in hand somehow?

God goes on to take full responsibility for the processes Job has raged about, but he suggests that Job has misunderstood the situation badly:

Have you entered the storehouses of the snow
or seen the storehouses of the hail,
which I reserve for times of trouble,
for days of war and battle?
What is the way to the place where the lightning is dispersed,
or the place where the east winds are scattered over the earth?
Who cuts a channel for the torrents of rain,
and a path for the thunderstorm,
to water a land where no one lives,
an uninhabited desert,
to satisfy a desolate wasteland
and make it sprout with grass?[17]

Here, God turns Job's argument on its head. These events do not show a lack of control; they are actually how God brings about his plans. Job has seen them as individual, one-off uncertainties. He has seen them as uncontrolled events which terrorize mankind. God, though, is saying that they are not isolated instances at all; he is painting a bigger picture. The apparent randomness on the smaller scale is combining to form the order which emerges for creation as a whole. Job's field of vision is far too narrow. God is telling him to widen it.

Is this realistic, though? Can God really be claiming that the disasters Job has identified are actually adding up to make our world a stable and predictable one to live in? Is this not just a case of an ancient text making excuses for its primitive "god"? What does our modern understanding of earth sciences have to say about this idea of an emergent "order" in nature?

Robert White is one of the foremost geophysicists in the world. A professor at Cambridge University and Fellow of the Royal Society, he has studied the questions in the previous paragraph in great detail. Writing down some of his findings in the book *Who Is To Blame?* he states that:

Natural processes such as earthquakes, volcanic eruptions, floods and the natural greenhouse effect are what make this world a fertile place in which to live. Without them, it would become a dead, sterile world and no one would be here to see it.[18]

God's proposition to Job millennia ago has been verified by the most up-to-date science we have. The Bible teaches that God has made a world in which uncertainty and chance – from our point of view –

operate at local level in order to produce a functioning, habitable world overall.

Job had tried to link God's failings in nature to his failings in the moral sphere. God picks apart the first of these accusations, encouraging Job to look deeper to find the truth. It is too simplistic, he says, to look at nature events in isolation and accuse him of not knowing best. The book of Isaiah revisits this principle, and has God saying:

> Though the mountains be shaken and the hills be removed, yet
> my unfailing love for you will not be shaken.[19]

As far as the Bible is concerned, God is in reliable control of our world, even if individual events might seem to suggest otherwise. When apparent randomness threatens to *destroy man's hope*, it calls us to hold on in the belief that God is painting a better big picture.

So key is this message throughout Scripture that we see some of its holiest characters taking it very deeply to heart, sometimes in the most moving of ways. The prophet Habakkuk is one of them. His belief that the big-picture God is good enables him to deal with the struggles of uncertainty:

> Though the fig-tree does not bud
> and there are no grapes on the vines,
> though the olive crop fails
> and the fields produce no food,
> though there are no sheep in the sheepfold
> and no cattle in the stalls,
> yet I will rejoice in the Lord,
> I will be joyful in God my Saviour.[20]

Putting Things Together

In Chapter 2, we looked at the science story over the ages, travelling backwards in time. Our first, most modern encounter was that of the mysterious jelly which seemed to form itself. The mystery was solved when it was realized that billions of bumbling peptides had managed to glue themselves together into tapes. Their rapid, erratic motion was crucial to this: only by crashing around haphazardly would they eventually build up any kind of emergent structure.

This is true over and over again at the microscopic scale. Countless biological processes depend on the wild frenzy of particle collisions.

As the particles wheel around crazily, they are effectively "exploring" every possible shape or material combination. Those that are even slightly more likely will end up as heavily favoured.

The result of all this "randomness" is the formation of cell walls, the maintenance of correct chemical concentrations, overwhelming victories for the immune system and more. It is from within all the chaos that overall order is formed – and life exists.

Modern scientists have learned that randomness and predictability are two sides of the same coin. When they see an event that is the product of chance, they do not conclude that there has been a loss of overall control. The apparently random behaviour of our weather, for example, is known to be channelled by reliable mechanisms, even if we are not ourselves privy to the outcome. The inherent uncertainty of quantum mechanics runs the same computer circuitry that we use to study it further.

These are lessons that the Bible has taught for centuries. When "freak" events make their appearances, we are not to think that God is out of control. He is the painter of a bigger picture and he invites us to see it for ourselves.

If our world was entirely random or entirely predictable, life as we know it would not be possible, and we could have no hope of any meaningful interaction with either nature or its Creator. We are told in the Bible that God has made it neither of these: he is found in both the chaos of the storm and the certainty of his love. This is spelled out in wonder as the psalmist describes the parting of the Red Sea:

> With your mighty arm you redeemed your people,
> the descendants of Jacob and Joseph.
>
> The waters saw you, God,
> the waters saw you and writhed;
> the very depths were convulsed.
> The clouds poured down water,
> the heavens resounded with thunder;
> your arrows flashed back and forth.
> Your thunder was heard in the whirlwind,
> your lightning lit up the world;
> the earth trembled and quaked.
> Your path led through the sea,
> your way through the mighty waters,
> though your footprints were not seen.
> You led your people like a flock.[21]

The Bible describes a God who uses randomness and predictability together in the rescue of the oppressed and hopeless. The terror of thunderstorm and earthquake result in the safety of a promised *path*.

We have seen in this chapter that the key ideas of chaos theory, statistical mechanics, and quantum mechanics are all in agreement with Guildenstern: the fact that chance exists in our world really does lead to *harmony* and *confidence*. Christians are in no way surprised by this. They trust in a steadfast God, one who calls them to believe that he rules over all their uncertainties. He calls them to believe that he is able to bring about, in their lives, what we have learned he brings about in nature: order from chaos.

7

QUESTIONS AND ANSWERS

Judge a man by his questions rather than by his answers.

Voltaire

When we use old confessions and catechisms, we help teach our people that their faith is an old faith, shared by millions over many centuries. We also help them realize that other Christians have asked the same questions.

Kevin DeYoung

Home science experiments for children are, thankfully, easier to access and explore than they have perhaps ever been. Budding engineers are only a click away from DIY hovercrafts, volcanoes, rockets, and lava lamps; fledgling chemists can make their own "slime", "magic mud", or even "elephant toothpaste". Admittedly, some of these projects are rather ambitious and come with the associated risk of strained family relationships or expensive cleaning bills. Happily though, others are interesting but straightforward. Take the following set of instructions, for example:

Start with an empty cardboard box. A round oatmeal box works well.

Punch a hole in the centre of the bottom by pushing a pencil through it.

Now place a piece of waxed paper over the open end of the box and hold it there with tape or a rubber band.

Your pinhole camera is complete.[1]

This pinhole camera is a curious object. Light travels into it through the small opening in one side and forms an image on the opposite side. The oddly enchanting image is of the outside world in full detail; yet it is both upside down and in miniature. The basic design and ease of use have made this device a highly popular craft activity for the young, but we should not be fooled by its simplicity. The pinhole camera has long been a source of both fascination and study for some of the greatest minds in history.

The effect was first mentioned by the influential Chinese philosopher Mozi (470–391 BC), who described the dark space in which the image formed as a "locked treasure room".[2] Many of the others to have spent time and words on the topic are familiar to us: Aristotle, Euclid, Robert Grosseteste, Roger Bacon, and Johannes Kepler have all weighed in.[3] All of these thinkers, Mozi included, clearly felt that the pinhole camera's image held within it deep wisdom about nature.

Between them, they discussed topics including geometry, optics, cosmology, the speed of light, and how the eye works – all by referencing this simple box. During the Renaissance, artists also discovered that the camera could help them produce a realistic sense of depth in their work; one sixteenth-century book recommended it "if you cannot paint". The strength of the hold that the device had on the creative scientific intellect is wonderfully summed up by none other than Leonardo da Vinci (1452–1519):

> Who would believe that so small a space could contain the image of all the universe? O mighty process! What talent can avail to penetrate a nature such as these? What tongue will it be that can unfold so great a wonder? Verily, none! This it is that guides the human discourse to the considering of divine things.[4]

It is now that we need to address something rather strange. Despite the fact that chemicals called silver nitrate and silver chloride had been synthesized in the thirteenth and sixteenth centuries respectively; despite the fact that they had both been shown to be responsive to light; despite the fact that some of the most creatively intelligent people who have ever lived had studied the pinhole camera almost to exhaustion; despite everything necessary for the process being firmly in place; *no one thought to take a photograph with it until 1850.*

This is extraordinary. If even one person had put the camera and chemical functions together before then, modern textbooks might hold photographs of Newton, Galileo, and Kepler. We might have had real images of the Great Fire of London, of Guy Fawkes being led off after his failed gunpowder plot, of William Shakespeare writing *Hamlet*. The history of photography – and, with it, the history of history – could have been so very different.

This can serve to remind us of one of the most vital lessons in science: it is not always the right answer that is missing. After all, everything needed for photography was present. More often than not, it is the right *question* that is desperately needed. The need for good questions in science will be the subject of this chapter. And, for proof of this, let us begin with a more successful photography story.

From the Mouths of Babes

Edwin H. Land (1909–91) was a born inventor. A chemist by training, he was interested in the properties of light and the technologies associated with it. Talented and inquisitive, he had enough early success in the field to found his own manufacturing company.

Land is now remembered primarily for his greatest invention of all: an instant camera that would become world famous. Yet, in a story related by the author Warren Berger, we discover something intriguing about this device.[5] Land, it is revealed, owed the groundbreaking idea to a three-year-old.

During a 1943 family holiday, Land took some photographs of his young daughter, Jennifer. Excited, she wanted to see the end result. Her father gently explained the need for patience; she could look at them later, after an in-store technician had developed the film. It was then that little Jennifer uttered the words that changed photography forever: "Why do we have to wait for the picture?"

Stopped in his tracks, Land realized that there was actually no binding scientific reason for having to take photos to a shop for development. Four years later, he had perfected a working model that would develop the pictures itself, as soon they were taken. His company – Polaroid – soon made these new-fangled machines available to the public: they sold out their entire stock on the first day of sales. Reflecting on this, Berger sees Land's story as typical:

> In my research, I've come across many breakthrough ideas or new ways of thinking that can be traced back to a beautiful question.

In the remainder of this chapter, then, we will recount four more science stories in which "beautiful" questions have resulted in new wisdom about nature. Having built the case that, in many ways, questions are actually more important than answers, we shall then investigate the attitude towards questioning in the world of the Christian faith. What, if anything, does the Bible have to say about questions? Could it be, as we have already seen in other areas, that having a Christian worldview is advantageous for the scientist?

Einstein, Again

Albert Einstein is certainly vying with Job for the title of most-mentioned person in this book. But why does he crop up again and again? What exactly was the secret of his amazing ability to advance our understanding of the universe? Clearly, he possessed a powerful intelligence; but what seems to raise him a level above most others is his lifelong tendency to ask new and unusual questions. He was well aware of this himself, telling *LIFE* magazine in 1955: "The important thing is not to stop questioning. Curiosity has its own reasons for existence."[6]

It has become rather fashionable in books about his life to tell the "story" of Einstein and the clock tower. He had, as the tale goes, a daily journey past a clock tower in his home town of Bern as part of his commute. One day, it continues, this inspired him to ask a life-changing question: "What would that clock look like if I was moving away from it at light speed?"

Despite its popularity, there is little evidence for the truth of this tale. In a strangely heart-warming way, it provides an insight into the humanity of the science community: it is as prone to romantic embellishment as any other.[7] What we definitely do know, however, is that in the period around winter 1895, Einstein was somehow driven to ask what would happen "if one were to run after a light wave with light velocity".[8]

He found that the mathematical answer to this was both odd and confusing. Ten years later, it had evolved into his theory of special relativity, with general relativity (Chapter 5) soon to follow. Einstein had asked the right question, and a new era of science was on its way.

This happens over and over again; great questions are the lifeblood of science. They can lead any potential answerer down a fresh, untrodden path of thought. A second startling example can be found in a scientific crossover point – one in which physics, chemistry, and biology all have their roles to play – biomedical engineering.

Making Cancer Worse

Cancer is undoubtedly one of the great scourges of life. Unsurprisingly, nearly all attempts to combat it have centred on destroying, shrinking, or containing tumours in some way. Yet a recent development has sprung from a shockingly different tactic: doing the complete opposite.

This sounds absurd. The fact is, though, that radically questioning the norm can open doors into previously unexplored rooms – and sometimes those rooms hold the answer. Knowing this, Dr Ravi Bellamkonda and his team of bioengineers at Georgia Institute of Technology dared to ask something truly bizarre: could they treat tumours by helping them grow?[9] Astonishingly, in 2014, they announced a new successful technique for treating the most feared of brain cancers. But how?

Bellamkonda's team had looked at the growth patterns of certain deadly tumours and found that they tended to snake along the brain's blood vessels or nerves. The scientists realized that they might be able guide this growth themselves by using synthetic fibres that "looked" like blood vessels to the cancer. Sure enough, these engineered strings proved irresistible, and the cancerous lump duly followed their man-made paths.

By positioning their artificial blood vessels carefully, the medics could lead the tumour steadily out of the brain into a toxic gel, where it would meet its doom. Cancer was being killed because someone had asked a new and potentially crazy question. Not all instances of crazy questioning, however, have results that are quite so meaningful...

Levitating Frogs

Nobel Prize-winning scientists are few and far between. In fact, only 200 have ever received the prize for physics. It is to one of them – Manchester University's Andre Geim – that we shall turn for our third example of novel questioning. When it comes to thinking outside the box, Geim is one of the very best.

Our story begins with curiosity and scepticism combined. Geim had heard that many companies were selling magnets which could be attached to household taps, with the promise that they would prevent the build-up of limescale. Intrigued (and dubious), Geim discovered fairly quickly that no one really knew all that much about the relationship between water and magnetism. Past theoretical work on the topic had been complicated, inconclusive, and (largely) fruitless. If these wonder products really did what they said – and it was far from clear that they did – no one was able to give a convincing reason for it.

Had it been anyone other than Geim taking an interest, the odds are that not much else would have happened. There might possibly have been another scientific paper written with a few more calculations, referencing work which had mentioned some sort of effect in the past. Geim, though, asked a different question. When wondering about "magnetic water", he did not simply study the literature and do some more sums. He asked what would happen if he just *did it*.

> With this idea in mind and, allegedly, on a Friday night, I poured water inside the lab's electromagnet when it was at its maximum power. Pouring water in one's equipment is certainly not a standard scientific approach, and I cannot recall why I behaved so "unprofessionally". Apparently, no one had tried such a silly thing before, although similar facilities existed in several places around the world for decades.[10]

It might seem unbelievable that a water-and-magnetism debate had gone on for so long without anyone actually trying it out, but genuinely brilliant questions often have that "why didn't I think of that?" quality. Gratifyingly, Geim's no-nonsense, *unprofessional* approach really paid off:

> As a result, we saw balls of levitating water. This was awesome... Many colleagues, including those who worked with high magnetic fields all their lives, were flabbergasted, and some of them even argued that this was a hoax.

A hoax it was not. Geim had shown that a property of water called "diamagnetism" could become strong enough to overcome gravity, suspending gobbets of it in the air. Geim's cult hero status was secured forever when he decided that the whole thing needed even more theatre: he floated a live frog (unharmed) and then released the video footage worldwide.

This experience never left his mind. Geim decided to build his career by hopping from discipline to discipline, each time asking new, crazy questions. Time and again, he was able to open doors no one else had even seen. This culminated in him finding a consistent method (which initially involved sticky tape) for manufacturing "graphene" – a super-material that will revolutionize electronics – and, with it, the 2010 Nobel Prize.

Geim would no doubt approve, then, of our chapter's next – and final – science story, the ramifications of which are huge. A thoroughly modern tale, it opens up the genuine possibility that we might, in the not-too-distant future, see teenagers with no formal scientific training on the Nobel stage. It is one which, like God's invitation to Job, really shows that science is for everyone.

From the Mouths of Babes II: This Time it's Digital

Amino acids are small organic molecules, made up of a handful of atoms. When they are glued together end-to-end they can form long protein chains: giant versions of our old friends, the peptides. Proteins have proved to be vital to all the life we know about. We can hear echoes of May's animal population work (complexity from simplicity) in the following description from science journal *Nature*:

> [proteins] serve as the catalysts for virtually every biochemical
> reaction that occurs in living things. This incredible array of
> functions derives from a startlingly simple code.[11]

To really understand a protein, however, it is not enough to know what it is made of. This is because these long chains always fold up, forming rich, three-dimensional objects. The intricate way each unique protein contorts itself into its final shape dictates both its behaviour and role.

Unless microbiologists know how a particular protein folds up, then, their knowledge is woefully incomplete; they are effectively studying in the dark. And, all too often, this is precisely where they find themselves.

The problem is this: there are just far too many folding possibilities. Any one protein chain could crease, crinkle, or bend in millions of different ways. Some of the end products can be easily discounted, but finding the one correct answer from those that remain can involve thousands and thousands of scientist-hours. It sounds like an ideal job for a computer, but programmers have found that certain types of shape-manipulation tasks are overwhelmingly tough for even our best machines. Protein folding turns out to be one of them.

Professor David Baker, a biochemist, had already explored the computational route. The program he had been using had been causing frustration. Sometimes, a better solution was available than the one shown on screen, but the machine did not select it, and Baker could not step in to overrule. It was then that he was inspired to ask a superb question: what if protein folding could be made into a computer game?

Thanks to the help of some colleagues in the Computer Science department, the folding problem was soon rewritten as a game called *FoldIt*. In 2008, it was given a free public online release.[12] Players could virtually fold up proteins and were awarded points for how well their attempts matched the key principles biochemists were already well aware of. High scores were stored on the web for all to see.

The outcome was extraordinary. In the most headline-grabbing case, *FoldIt* gamers managed to find the correct structure of an AIDS-related virus that had remained a mystery for thirteen years – and they did it in just ten days. In the resulting paper, Baker and his team state the following:

> The refined structure provides new insights for the design of retro-viral drugs… These results indicate the potential for integrating video games into the real-world scientific process: the ingenuity of game players is a formidable force that, if properly directed, can be used to solve a wide range of scientific problems.[13]

The beauty of Baker's simple question is that it draws so imaginatively on the humanness of science we discussed in Chapter 3. He has (along with Geim, Bellamkonda, Einstein, and Jennifer Land) shown decisively that a good question can sometimes make far more difference than a good answer.

Answers tend to complete a process or concept, but questions begin new ones. With this idea in place, let us move on in the only way that seems appropriate, and ask something: if having an attitude of constant questioning is indeed a necessary quality for the scientist, can *faith* help?

To Question or Not to Question

We have dealt previously with the claim Richard Dawkins has popularized about "faith-heads" – that those in faith communities actually celebrate having a closed mind, seeing it as a virtue rather than a weakness. We found, in Chapter 4, that this contrasted dramatically with the biblical instruction to *seek out* wisdom as well as with the mental about-face required for conversion. Now, though, we face a similar but slightly different issue: does Christianity tell its adherents not to ask questions?

A.N. Wilson is a Fellow of the Royal Society of Literature and one of the most senior literary figures living in Britain today. In 1992, he wrote a book entitled *Jesus*, in which he sought to strip away the religious "mythology" surrounding the real historical person.

Wilson argued that Jesus was merely a man, and dismissed any notions of deity or a greater supernatural reality. In a newspaper interview carried out that year, he theorizes that followers of Jesus Christ would realize the truth themselves if they actually gave it any thought:

> "When Christians start thinking about Jesus," says Wilson, "things start breaking down, they lose their faith. It's perfectly possible to go to church every Sunday and not ask any questions, just because you like it as a way of life. They fear that if they ask questions they'll lose their Christ."[14]

This sounds broadly familiar. We have heard before that faith-heads are immune to argument and evidence; Wilson adds that they refuse to ask questions. Is this a fair assessment? As we have pointed out already, statements like this might well be an accurate description of some individuals identifying as Christians; but that is not the same thing as describing Christianity itself. By now, this much should be obvious: if we want to know what the attitude of Christians should be, we need to consult the Bible.

From our journey so far, we are well aware that the book of Job is stacked full of questions, many of which come from God himself. We have seen that these questions often have a scientific flavour and that they are invitational. God asks these questions in a way that pushes Job (and us) to think deeper. We are to ask these questions, and others like them, for ourselves.

Far from being exclusive to Job, though, questioning is a biblical pattern. There are 66 books in the Bible, giving nearly 1,200 chapters overall, and these contain, between them, a staggering 3,300 questions.[15] Getting to know them is the work of a lifetime; but we can begin to get a feel by considering just a few.

Where are You?

The question in this heading is the very first to appear in the biblical text. Found in the book of Genesis, it is asked of Adam and Eve, by God. Embedded within the story of the Fall, it is a powerful example of just what God's questioning is designed to do: get us to really think. Adam and Eve had rejected God – his wisdom, love, and authority – by rebelling against him and disobeying his instruction. The immediate aftermath provides the context for our question:

> Then the man and his wife heard the sound of the Lord God as he was walking in the garden in the cool of the day, and they hid from the Lord God among the trees of the garden. But the Lord God called to the man, "Where are you?"[16]

Why did God ask this? It cannot be that he did not know the answer already; the Bible consistently presents him as all-knowing. God knows precisely where Adam and Eve are, and he knows exactly what has happened. Clearly, his question has a different, deeper purpose.

God is pushing Adam and Eve to consider gravely the state they now find themselves in: hidden from their Maker, relationally damaged. He asks about their circumstances so that they will start asking about those circumstances themselves. From the very beginning, the Bible teaches us that God's questions are not there to silence us; instead, they are designed to lead to our own.

How Long, Lord?

When we last encountered the prophet Habakkuk in Chapter 6, he was professing his faith in God's ability to bring order from chaos. What was not mentioned back then, though, is that this declaration was the final result of a question-and-answer session with God himself. The Old Testament book Habakkuk contains the full exchange, and it opens with the prophet interrogating his Creator:

> How long, Lord, must I call for help,
> but you do not listen?
> Or cry out to you, "Violence!"
> but you do not save?
> Why do you make me look at injustice?
> Why do you tolerate wrongdoing?[17]

These are forceful and direct questions about the sorry moral state of the Israelites from a lowly man to the Almighty. Should we now expect a divine fist to crash down from heaven and flatten Habakkuk for his insolence? What does God think of his people when they challenge him like this?

> Look at the nations and watch –
> and be utterly amazed.
> For I am going to do something in your days
> that you would not believe,
> even if you were told.
> I am raising up the Babylonians,
> that ruthless and impetuous people.[18]

What better sign could there be that God approves of questioning – even questioning that accuses him of wrongdoing – than for him to answer? Habakkuk clearly sees this as encouragement to keep going, and so he does. He is outraged that God might be about to administer justice to the Israelites via the *Babylonians* (who he sees as even worse) so he complains for a second time.

Once again, God gives him an answer. At the end of the three-chapter dialogue, Habakkuk's worries are gone. God has convinced him that all is truly in hand and that big-picture goodness will emerge from writhing moral disorder. The final outcome is the strengthening of Habakkuk's faith, the evidence for which we have come across before:

> though there are no sheep in the pen
> and no cattle in the stalls,
> yet I will rejoice in the Lord,
> I will be joyful in God my Saviour.[19]

Who Do You Say I Am?

The centrepiece of the whole Bible is the ministry, death, and resurrection of Jesus Christ. The Old Testament looks forward to it; the New Testament analyses it. Ultimately, the Bible revolves entirely around this one Person. The constant proclamation is that Jesus is divine, that the Creator of our world also entered into it, taking on a human nature. As we will see further in Chapter 9, Christianity stands or falls on the true identity of Jesus, because the Bible is unequivocal:

he is God. Paul writes of the glorious Jesus he encountered on the Damascus road:

> He is the image of the invisible God, the firstborn over all creation. For in him all things were created: things in heaven and on earth, visible and invisible, whether thrones or powers or rulers or authorities; all things have been created through him and for him. He is before all things, and in him all things hold together.[20]

The Christian, therefore, believes that God is seen in Jesus. The Creator has shown himself in real-world history. God's personality, priorities, passions, and principles can be known by studying the life and teaching of Jesus. If a Christian wants to know what God thinks about an issue, he or she will find answers in the words and actions of Jesus; and these are found in his biographies, the Gospels. So what does God – Jesus – think about the importance of questions?

The four Gospels (Matthew, Mark, Luke, and John) each give accounts of Jesus' time on earth. They tell of his miracles, his sermons, and his day-to-day interactions with society. And, significantly for us, they also record him asking questions – more than 300 of them.

Centuries earlier God had questioned Job, Adam, and Eve with the aim of getting them to ask their own questions. In Jesus, he was now doing same for anyone willing to listen. Jesus was not asking for the sake of gaining information, he was pushing people to question themselves. Understanding that puts a different spin entirely on the sort of things he asked:

Why are you so afraid?[21]

Why do you entertain evil thoughts in your hearts?[22]

Do you believe that I am able to do this?[23]

Why did you doubt?[24]

What good will it be for a man if he gains the whole world, yet forfeits his soul?[25]

Why do you ask me about what is good?[26]

Can any of you prove me guilty of sin?[27]

Don't you know me, even after I have been among you such a long time?[28]

Jesus' questioning calls on people to think. He believes that questions open up new doors and bring about profound change. This is consistent with the overall biblical picture. Where, then, does our analysis of questioning in the Scriptures leave us? What should be the Christian attitude towards asking questions? Is questioning wrong? Should Christians be afraid to ask to questions – as A.N. Wilson suggested they usually were?

The Bible would say not. In its pages, we find God asking questions; we find God leading humanity into doing the same; we find God encouraging questioning by entering into dialogue; we find God, in human form, using questions to teach. We are left with only one reasonable conclusion: Christians – literally "little Christs" – should have questioning hardwired into their very life. After all, it is a new life, and it began with a question:

"But what about you?" Jesus asked. "Who do you say I am?"[29]

Addressing the Whole

While on the topic of new life, let us return to A.N. Wilson. We encountered him earlier as an avowed atheist, writing at length that Jesus was most certainly not God. Wilson, though, has changed his mind.

He now asserts "a belief in the risen Christ". He says his previous, godless stance "simply won't do – on an intellectual level". Following in the footsteps of Paul, he has moved from attacking Jesus to confessing him as God. To what, exactly, does Wilson attribute this most dramatic of reversals?

Given the content of this chapter, we should not be surprised to find that his answer is *questions*. The more he asked about life, the more he found himself convinced by the biblical claims about Jesus. Describing his struggles with the same apparent injustice that had moved Habakkuk, Job, and Asaph, Wilson says:

Easter does not answer such questions by clever-clever logic. Nor is it irrational. On the contrary, it meets our reason and our hearts together, for it addresses the whole person. In the past, I have questioned its veracity and suggested that it should not be taken literally. But the more I read the Easter story, the better it seems to fit and apply to the human condition. That, too, is why I now believe in it.[30]

Wilson found that the Bible spoke to his emotions and to his intellect; it *addresses the whole*. This is the joined-up thinking that the Christian faith can provide. In placing such a high value on questioning, it prepares Christians for all aspects of life.

Questions lift our eyes from the narrow tracks we walk on. They lead us to make creative connections. They make us think about relationships between things, and between us, others and the world. People who ask questions are well equipped. They are equipped to fold proteins, equipped to fight cancer, and – most wonderfully of all – they are equipped to *know God.*

8

LOVE

My first crush was Spock. I thought it didn't get any better than Spock.

Selma Blair

And yet I will show you the most excellent way.

The apostle Paul

Time and again, we have found it appropriate to describe both the giant leaps and the small steps in the history of science as *stories*. It seems that any study of the way the world works necessarily involves the ups and downs of our humanity. Discoveries come via wonder or frustration, curiosity or stubbornness, pain or hope. Science, we have found, is just as much about *people* as it is about process.

This constant interplay of human personality and scientific enquiry has resulted in many profound realizations about our universe, as we have seen. Real science is rarely, if ever, confined to just systematic, fact-gathering investigation. Without the deeply human traits of imagination, creativity and playful experimentation, we would know almost nothing. For this reason, even three-year-olds can shape the future of technology, as Chapter 7 showed.

Genuine and effective scientific thought should not, therefore, be pictured as a *canal*, a waterway of austere straight lines, mechanically constructed with fixed and rigid destinations in mind. It is much more like a *river*, with gradually evolving meanders and tributaries, continually interacting with its wider environment. Sometimes this river bursts its banks entirely and spreads out into other human fields. As a result, it has flooded – among others – literature, stage, art, film, television, and computer gaming. In fact, this overflow has given rise to an entire genre: science *fiction*.

As a rich blend of human thinking and imagination, science fiction allows authors, screenwriters, or developers to ask "what if…?" and then explore an almost limitless set of answers. In sci-fi, anything goes. The conventional understanding of time or of space or of our place in the cosmos can be rewritten or even bypassed entirely.

Alien life forms can become key characters; some are almost human, while others stretch the definition of "life" to breaking point. Androids and artificial intelligences rival or surpass our own capabilities. And, of course, there is the beloved theme of time travel, leading to plots with even more holes in them than quantum mechanical space–time.

Many fans of sci-fi will have a favourite novel, character, machine, realm, or episode. Some discuss these alternate realities at length, some write their own additional fan fiction, and others engage in role playing. Yet, despite having to compete in a huge and congested field, certain stories still manage to stand out. And when it comes to innovative science, public profile, and longevity – love it or hate it – few worlds can rival that of *Star Trek*.

First conceived by Gene Roddenberry (1921–91) in the mid-1960s, *Star Trek* has spawned six different TV series, twelve feature films (with at least two more on the way at the time of writing), and hundreds of novels, comics, and video games. The secret of its success seems to be the way in which it revels in both scientific ingenuity and human drama.

Technical descriptions of transporter malfunctions are as much a part of the story as the brash arrogance of Captain James T. Kirk. Detailed analyses of space–time anomalies sit happily alongside the political soul-searching of Captain Jean-Luc Picard. Assorted alien races and individuals bring with them even more complex technologies and personalities. One of these aliens appears to have captured the imagination more than the countless others found in the *Star Trek* universe: Captain Kirk's First Officer, Mr Spock.

The popularity of Spock as a character could be considered a little surprising. Half-human, half-Vulcan, it was decided after a pilot episode that Spock should be primarily a logical being, always seeking to suppress emotion. His would be the voice of detached reason. Feelings such as frustration, anxiety, anger, joy, or excitement were not to influence his decision-making or, as a Starfleet officer, his advice to Kirk. Rational, unsympathetic, mathematical rigour was to be the order of Spock's day. Despite this pre-planned immovability, Spock went on to be one of the most-loved figures in the franchise – because he was ultimately portrayed as a man facing an inner battle.

Spock's emotionless existence was different from that of a computer. On one level he was indeed a processing machine, operating without sentiment, but this was not explained by an inherent lack of emotional capacity. Instead, the writers had Spock taking this stance on principle.

In his Vulcan thinking, Spock considered romanticism or zeal of any kind as distracting or even dangerous: it could only get in the way of making the best possible call in any situation. His focus on logic was therefore deliberate. The attraction of Spock, though, is due to the nagging internal tension tied up in his decision to live this way. We always get the sense that possibly, very deep down, Spock *knows* he is missing out, and missing out on something that is far more profound than his pure, stripped-down reason.

One example of this is found in "The Lights of Zetar", an episode from the original series.[1] Scotty, the ship's engineer, has fallen for a colleague. His devotion to her ultimately saves her from death, against all the odds, when others had long since given up. As they review these events, Kirk asks Spock whether he thinks, perhaps, it was Scotty's *love* for his teammate that made the difference. For just a second, Spock appears to waver. He allows himself to wonder whether humans really might be correct in attributing so much to "that emotion". It is only a moment, yes – but it is a telling one.

It is precisely these sorts of instances that let us in, however briefly, on Spock's niggling doubts. Is machine-like rationalism really the best way? Could emotional commitment help us achieve great things that logic – on its own – could not? Are humans right to place so much emphasis on the extraordinary power of love?

Maybe Spock had been studying these questions in his own time, seeking to become a more effective Science Officer, wondering if love could hold the key, even to scientific matters. Of course, as a logical being, he would have studied, in detail, those things which have had the deepest influence on the humans he was trying to understand. Spock might have worked his way through poetry, music, art, and more in his quest to place a value on love – and, sooner or later, his search would have led him, logically, to the most influential text of them all: the Bible.

The Greatest of These

If he had indeed searched through the Scriptures, Spock would have found plenty to go on: love is a favourite topic of the Bible. Its pages have much to say on what love is, how it shows itself, and why it matters. Love is key to the biblical big picture; it underpins the right relationships offered to us with God, with each other, with ourselves, and with nature. A few passages are particularly worth studying, so we shall do so and then return to the theme of Vulcan angst, hopefully with some useful lessons in tow.

The Bible is abundantly clear throughout in saying that no person, object, or quality is deserving of worship except God himself, a fact we first noted in Chapter 4. Despite this, we saw that it readily exalts and even personifies wisdom as something to be greatly treasured. Such high esteem for wisdom, however, pales in comparison with the biblical treatment of love. The apostle John, one of Jesus' closest companions during his earthly ministry, goes so far as to write: "God is love."[2]

John could have said "God is loving", but he pushes the connection even deeper, identifying God as love itself. At first, a reader might interpret this statement as being rather wishy-washy. Where is the powerful, nature-wielding Supreme Being we read of in Job? The line "God is love" summons up images of tie-dye T-shirts, interpretative dance, or scatter cushions. Where are the earthquakes, thunderstorms, or sovereign rule over the universe?

John, however, does not have a soft, mushy sort of love in mind. Instead, the love he extols is potent and formidable and active. In his Gospel account, John recalls the teaching that Jesus gave to his disciples:

My command is this: Love each other as I have loved you. Greater love has no one than this: to lay down one's life for one's friends.[3]

Here, God – in the person of Jesus – says he is the origin and example of true love. This love is selfless and sacrificial, it is loyal and steadfast, and it is demonstrated powerfully by Jesus in his death on the cross. This is a love that takes a stand when it matters. It is the love of a family or community, with each individual putting the others first. The apostle Paul was profoundly impacted by the quality and power of the love he found flowing from Jesus:

Love is patient, love is kind. It does not envy, it does not boast, it is not proud. It does not dishonour others, it is not self-seeking, it is not easily angered, it keeps no record of wrongs. Love does not delight in evil but rejoices with the truth. It always protects, always trusts, always hopes, always perseveres.
Love never fails.[4]

The word translated as *protects* in this passage is also found in the name of the dinosaur *Stegosaurus*, in which it indicates the rugged toughness of the giant animal's armour plating. The impression Paul wants the reader to receive is that real love can take a real beating and yet still keep going. John agrees – he spells this out in his own letters, calling Christians to follow the example of their Christ:

> This is how we know what love is: Jesus Christ laid down his life for us. And we ought to lay down our lives for our brothers and sisters. If anyone has material possessions and sees a brother or sister in need but has no pity on them, how can the love of God be in that person? Dear children, let us not love with words or speech but with actions and in truth.[5]

This last line is particularly worth noting: love involves both *actions* and *truth*. The former implies committed selflessness, as addressed above; but what about the latter? Sometimes, seeking *truth* means challenging a currently held view, even a deep one, as Chapter 4 reminded us. It might mean having to change that view. In fact, John sees the correction of error as a vital aspect of love. This key point is also found in the Old Testament book Proverbs, and it is repeated in the New Testament in Hebrews:

> Do not despise the Lord's discipline, and do not resent his rebuke, because the Lord disciplines those he loves, as a father the son he delights in.[6]

The Bible is, ultimately, a love story. God – who *is* love – creates humanity to live in loving relationship with him, and with each other, and with nature. Humanity then turns away, breaking each of these bonds. God enters into human life, personally, on a rescue mission. He, in Jesus, is crucified, taking upon himself the punishment for the rebellion. In doing so, he is *patient* and *kind* and he *keeps no record of wrongs* for those who want to come back to him.

In the passages above, we find a God who calls humans to love in the same active, powerful way he does. He encourages us to live out a loving interaction with him, each other, and nature, as things were supposed to be from the beginning. We are to look for (and enjoy) wisdom and beauty in each of these relationships, doing so as a family or community.

For the scientist, there is a particular affinity with the humans-with-nature relationship. What might applying biblical love look like in this case? Although we will consider the answer to this more fully in Chapter 10, some brief points are certainly worth making now. For instance, the loving scientist *hopes* and *perseveres*. He or she will be open to correction. He or she will be prepared to face the difficult times, even if that involves taking a temporary mental (and, usually, emotional) beating, as it did for some in the early days of quantum mechanics.

He or she will look primarily to the interests of others and, if necessary, adopt a sacrificial attitude for the greater good. The desire for individual praise or honour may have to be laid down in order to make overall progress through collaboration. These are just a few quick examples, but they do begin to show the possible gains of having love in the lab.

The Bible claims that God, being love, is the prototype for our own. This, Scripture says, is why love is so powerful: it is the reason we were created in the first place and, in turn, our own calling. Love is designed into us right from the start. Convinced of this, Paul finishes his analysis of love by looking forward to fully restored relationships, concluding:

> For now we see only a reflection as in a mirror; then we shall see face to face. Now I know in part; then I shall know fully, even as I am fully known.
>
> And now these three remain: faith, hope and love. But the greatest of these is love.[7]

An analysis of divine love is all well and good, and relating it to scientific enterprise gives some theoretical reasons for its value, but would this be enough for our logical friend Spock to reconsider his position? Granted, his study of the Scriptures would have been more thorough than our brief one, leading to an even richer view of the love of Jesus, but he would almost certainly want some concrete evidence. Is there any? Are there actually any real-world examples of science benefiting from love? Wonderfully, and perhaps surprisingly to some, it would appear that there are.

Being Wrongly Correct

Spock would be glad to know that our first science love story arises from the human desire to explore what *Star Trek* describes as the "Final Frontier": space. For as long as civilizations have been recording information, they have been studying the skies. Astronomy seems to be as old as we are. Obviously, all early observations were made without the aid of any imaging equipment, and would therefore have been carried out with the naked eye. For this reason, they tended to be dominated by the behaviour of the Sun and the Moon, with the stars often treated collectively as some sort of fixed backdrop.

A handful of special "stars", though, were clearly a little different from the others. They did not drift nicely along with the collective, but instead seemed to do their own individual thing. The Greeks called them "wanderers", or *planets*. Trying to figure out what exactly the relationship was between the Earth, Moon, Sun, planets, and stars became a favourite human exercise.

While there was certainly practical use (navigation, agriculture, and more) in knowing which heavenly bodies would do what, we can be fairly certain that much of the motivation came from that classic characteristic of humanity discussed in Chapter 3: a delight in wisdom about nature. As Ralph Waldo Emerson (1803–82), the American essayist, says: "Men love to wonder, and that is the seed of our science."[8]

Although some had suggested otherwise – most notably, some followers of Pythagoras (570–495 BC) – the general agreement in the ancient world was that the Earth was at the centre of the universe. This is not an unreasonable starting point at all: after all, we tend to think it about ourselves, too. It is also the way the sky "looks": there is no evidence presented to the eye (or to any of our sense organs, in fact) that the Earth might be whirling in a vast orbit about the Sun.

In this view, all other heavenly bodies would orbit the Earth, with the stars doing so as a group. The underlying assumptions were twofold: the Earth was stationary, and everything else would move round it in the most perfect shape of them all – a circle. Both Plato and Aristotle championed this approach. It is, as we now know, wrong.

Over time, as a wrong model is studied by enough people, inconsistencies will show up. In this case, the motion of the Sun became an issue. Observations showed that at some times it was nearer the Earth than at others. Similarly, the planets didn't play along: they even travelled "backwards" occasionally. Ptolemy (AD 100–170) bravely took both of these discrepancies on – and managed to find a solution.

He proposed that the centre of the Sun's circular orbit was not the Earth, but at another fixed point nearby. He suggested that the planets might be tracing out smaller mini-circles at the same time as following their main big one – like a teacup on a fairground ride – which explained their backwards "wobbling" from the Earth's perspective.

The resulting mathematical system allowed astronomers to keep their perfect circles and stationary Earth and, despite being wholly incorrect, it also matched the observational data tolerably well. In fact, Ptolemy's complex model was so good that it was accepted by almost every astronomer worldwide for more than a millennium. Overcoming its vice-like grip would take a labour of love.

Being Correctly Wrong

Occasional challenges to the Ptolemaic system arose, but it reigned supreme nonetheless. It was not until the work of Nicolaus Copernicus (1473–1543) that the process of dethroning it began in earnest. Copernicus pursued the same ideas raised by some of the Pythagoreans – that the Earth orbited the Sun.

Copernicus had one major advantage over Ptolemy: his model still used circles, but this time everything also moved at a steady, unchanging speed. This behaviour, called "uniform circular motion", was considered to be far more elegant than the Ptolemaic speeding up and slowing down – and in science, as in so many other areas, beautiful things are loved just that little bit more.

Copernicus correctly identified the Earth as a planet. He correctly stated that it orbited the Sun once a year and correctly described it as rotating on its own axis once a day. He called – again, correctly – for a Sun-centred (heliocentric) view to replace an Earth-centred (geocentric) view. This was, literally, revolutionary thinking.

Regardless of all this progress, though, the Copernican model (eventually published in 1543 AD)[9] had a potentially deadly flaw. For, despite the massive overhaul in thinking that he undertook and then expected of any disciples, Copernicus did not really match the observations any better than Ptolemy did.[10]

This is a point worth repeating, since it comes as a surprise to us: when the Polish astronomer's heliocentrism was formally introduced, it was no improvement, evidence-wise, on geocentrism. More too: it also required its would-be followers to believe that the earth was hurtling through space at incredible speed – something for which there was no obvious support.

How could any genuine natural philosopher accept this new condition honestly, when there was nothing to indicate its truth? Copernicus couldn't offer better agreement than Ptolemy, and yet his model demanded an unlikely and unsubstantiated fact to be accepted entirely on faith. This is pushing the scientific method to breaking point: as far as the results of the day were concerned, heliocentrism could only really be considered to be *wrong*.

How, then, could this demonstrably incorrect theory ever get off the ground? Who would be prepared to nurture it through these rocky early days? Who would see its beauty and choose to value that more highly than the data? Who would join Copernicus, and show it some *love*?

Don't Worry, it's Only a Phase

On top of all the talk about heliocentrism's failure to displace geocentrism, it is worth mentioning that both models had a major shortcoming. The problem was one of those pesky "wanderers": Venus. Ptolemy and Copernicus both had Venus' distance from the earth varying significantly during its orbit – which should have had a noticeable effect on how *bright* it appeared to be.

Instead, Venus seemed to stay pretty much the same brightness all year round. This didn't make sense, and called into question the basics of both systems – and people didn't talk about it much. Whilst it does not help us choose between theories, the Venus problem certainly highlights the great difficulties that there were in knowing what exactly *was* going on in the heavens. Any notions of cut and dried, neat and tidy answers are essentially pie in the sky – as we have already seen in many of our earlier science stories.

Let us be under no illusion: determining the structure of the solar system was no simple matter, and it would be foolish to suggest (as some now like to do with the benefit of hindsight) that the heliocentric truth was always clear for anyone to see. And yet, the idea of things being clear to see was what eventually resolved the whole puzzle: how was it that this feeble and anaemic sun-centred model ever got further than the drawing-board? Enter the great Italian experimentalist himself – Galileo.

We encountered Galileo previously in Chapter 2, exhorting would-be scientists to actually try things out. He would have undoubtedly approved of Andre Geim's decision to hurl water into his electromagnet, for instance. Galileo's relevance to our cosmic story is that he managed to solve the brightness problem – by looking through a telescope.

As he carefully watched Venus, Galileo noticed something wonderful. The planet appeared to *change shape*, and to do so in the most familiar of ways: Venus, it became clear, had *phases*. Just as the Moon (as Macrina pointed out in Chapter 2) is lit differently by the Sun – full circle, half, crescent, and so on – Venus would grow and then shrink. Sometimes, Galileo glimpsed just a sliver; sometimes, a gloriously full disc.

This was the death knell for Ptolemy. His model did not permit Venus to have phases, and it could not be modified to do so. The pendulum began to swing the way of Copernicus – and soon received yet another push in this direction.

Galileo showed that the near-constant brightness of Venus when viewed with the naked eye was indeed consistent with a sun-centred solar system. The planet was, in fact, moving nearer and then further, just as Copernicus had predicted – but this was being balanced by the phases. When Venus was far off, it was fully lit. When Venus was near, it was a mere shaving of light. The two effects cancelled out: the planet looked equally splendid at all times.

Since these phases of Venus were invisible to the naked eye, Copernicus (who didn't have a telescope) never knew about them. He had thrown himself into his work on heliocentrism despite its inherent weaknesses during his own lifetime. Like Ignaz Semmelweis and Robert Brown, Copernicus died before ever seeing the scientific resolution to his problem.

What, exactly, enables scientists to work with theories which seem woefully inadequate? Is it the detached, rational logic of Spock and of the so-called scientific method? Is it human gut instinct? Is it *love*?

Unscientific Progress

Is it exaggeration at best (and dishonesty at worst) to suggest that love plays any part in real scientific work? How could we possibly know whether emotional commitment of any sort was motivating Copernicus in his contemplation of the heavens? Is it not just the case that truth will always emerge if proper observations and analysis are allowed to run their course? After all, isn't this really a story of a telescope making the difference? As Tina Turner famously asked: "What's love got to do with it?"

In deciding what might have moved great scientists of the past, it would help our cause greatly to know if we can find evidence of humanity – and, hopefully of this biblical, active love – in modern investigation. The pioneers of today, as they consider the cutting-edge equivalents of heliocentrism, can be a primary source for our thinking about love and science. Let us consider a few examples and then revisit the Copernican Revolution with them in mind.

One technology that we can expect to see really explode over the next few decades is that of "bioresorbable" implants. These are devices that can be located anywhere in the body to deliver a treatment of some sort and then be absorbed through natural processes once their job is done; no surgery is required for their removal. Jen Thies works for Royal DSM (see Chapter 1) and is at the forefront of work on bioresorbables. He readily admits that selfless commitment is vital:

> I've learned that you've got to be in love with the problem, not just the solution.[11]

Brian Greene, the string theorist we encountered in Chapter 5, describes his working environment as a melting pot of rigorous thought and human feeling:

> Science is the process that takes us from confusion to understanding in a manner that's precise, predictive and reliable – a transformation, for those lucky enough to experience it, that is empowering and emotional.[12]

The world-famous physicist Stephen Hawking, who featured alongside Greene in our discussion of a Grand Unified Theory, agrees with him wholeheartedly:

> Humans are an adventurous species. We like to explore and are inspired by journeys to the unknown. Science is not only a disciple of reason but, also, one of romance and passion.[13]

Vilayanur S. Ramachandran, one of the most highly regarded neuroscientists in the world, was asked during a newspaper interview how he dealt with the continued demand to advance our understanding of the human brain. His response is telling:

> No pressure. I do what I want. The discoveries speak for themselves. The minute you succumb to outside pressure you cease to be creative. Science is like a love affair with nature; an elusive, tantalising mistress. It has all the turbulence, twists and turns of romantic love, but that's part of the game.[14]

Finally, Tim Harford, economist and journalist, points out that even those outside science can feel and benefit from the emotional involvement of those within it. He says of Professor Brian Cox, physicist and TV presenter:

> I don't think Brian Cox does "The Wonders of the Solar System" because he believes the world would be a better place if people understood about the rings of Saturn; I just think he finds physics extremely interesting. It brings him joy, and he wants to spread the love.[15]

There is an undeniable pattern here, and it is found right across ultra-modern science. It seems that the people in the trade really think that love is *needed*.

The love they describe is birthed by wonder and it is prepared to stand firm under testing. It is prepared to focus on the good when other results are not encouraging, and it is prepared to nurture struggling, incomplete ideas into fully grown models. Real scientific progress, it would appear, is dependent on this kind of love. Spock should take note. He may need to change his approach.

Loving Science

We shall finish this chapter by considering one final science love story: that of another space scientist, Professor Lawrence Krauss. Our first clue that Krauss might appreciate the human drama found in real science is that he has written a book entitled *The Physics of Star Trek*.[16] This seems like the work of a man who recognizes the winding river picture we began with.

Since the mid-1990s, Krauss has been promoting a theory about the future of the universe. He thinks that space will continue to expand for all time, but at an ever-decreasing rate. This theory, known as the "flat universe" model, has had a troubled life at times.

Experiments and data from past years have often made a flat universe seem very unlikely. When Krauss first threw his support behind it, he was swimming against the tide. Like Copernicus before him though, Krauss pushed strongly for his theory, despite a lack of evidential support:

> What Michael Turner and I argued in 1995 was heretical in the extreme. Based on little more than theoretical prejudice, we presumed the universe was flat... Our idea was crazy by any standards.[17]

The parallels with Copernicus continue. Krauss stuck by his idea, and it now seems that he may well be right after all. Technological advances have provided evidence that favours his stance. New, high-powered investigations have led NASA to back the flat model publicly,[18] and (bar the finer details) the physics community now broadly accepts this very special "universal flatness".

History appears to have repeated itself. Neither Copernicus nor Krauss had sufficient data on their side at first, but both championed their views regardless. Both were shown to be right when further experimentation unlocked new truths. Their nurturing of these fragile, unconvincing ideas and their willingness to take a beating in the process sounds much like the love that the Bible writers Paul and John spoke of.

Sometimes being scientific involves far more than detached logic. This point is made wonderfully by philosopher of science, Paul Feyerabend (1924–94):

> Copernicanism and other "rational" views exist today only because reason was overruled at some time in their past.[19]

Science, at its most successful, blends the 'gutsy love' of functional human relationships with rationality. What does this observation mean for a scientist who has a Christian faith? Do Christians have a monopoly on scientifically fruitful emotion?

No, of course not. Yet the Bible *does* call them to see love as their highest priority. It also insists that this love should be active, hopeful, determined, patient, and inspired by grand ideas. Does science benefit from those attitudes? It most certainly does – as we have seen. More than that, we have found that it is actually essential to science making any great progress.

What, then, should be our final guidance to Spock? Perhaps it would be fitting to refer him to that fellow explorer of space, Copernicus himself. He writes:

> To know the mighty works of God, to comprehend His wisdom and majesty and power; to appreciate, in degree, the wonderful workings of His laws, surely all this must be a pleasing and acceptable mode of worship to the Most High, to whom ignorance cannot be more grateful than knowledge.[20]

Emotion pours out of these words, which come from the pen of one of our greatest scientists. Spock should consider them very carefully. They are words of discovery, of truth, and of progress; they are words of *love*.

9

RECONCILIATION

Do not be afraid of being free thinkers. If you think strongly enough you will be forced by science to the belief in God.

Lord Kelvin

The God of the Bible is also the God of the genome. He can be worshipped in the cathedral or in the laboratory.

Francis Collins

We have been on quite a journey. The science stories we have dropped in on have been ancient and modern, profound and amusing, joyful and painful, complex and simple. Above all, they have been deeply and unmistakeably *human*. Despite the tendency to think of science as an almost otherworldly enterprise – a separate and distinct realm reserved for just a few, ruled by method, evidence, and logical progress – we have been reminded that it is, at heart, people being people.

Dead ends, painful mistakes, confusing results, and even contradictions all play their part. Irrational impulses, unjustifiable gut instincts, and steadfast love for flawed new ideas showing beauty or promise have brought forth fresh – and sometimes astonishing – understanding. Real science, like so many other human pursuits, is sometimes triumphant and sometimes a struggle. Even today, right at the very heart of physics, there is a fundamentally broken relationship, as we saw in Chapter 5 – and still, no one is quite sure how to fix it.

Alongside all these stories, we have considered the role and the value of the Christian faith and its core principles in the human pursuit of wisdom about nature. We have seen that Christianity does not shy away from discussing the reality of the difficulties we face. Instead, it offers resources and approaches that support the scientist on both good and bad days.

Christianity, like physics, also has broken relationship at its core. In fact, it has four of them, as we shall see. This time, though, the key to their resolution is no mystery. It is explained in detail and it is readily available. We have hinted at all of this before.

Now, however, it is time to bring the Christian message front and centre. We will look, in quite some depth, at what the Bible says is the story of humanity, told in terms of relationship. In doing so, we will find ourselves faced with a possibility that is of universal importance. Christianity, it seems, might just be able to tell us what science is *for*.

In the Beginning

The Bible teaches us, primarily, about God and about us. God, it says, is perfect. He is not perfect by some external measure, he himself is the measure. Real perfection, therefore, takes its very definition from who God is and from what he is like. With this in mind, it is significant to note that God is written about repeatedly both in the singular and in the plural. In fact, he is presented throughout Scripture as *three* distinct Persons in *one* single Being: the "Trinity".

The notion of the Trinity is mighty confusing to us humans since we, individually, each have a one-person-per-being structure. It is no surprise, then, that this doctrine was only formalized 300 years after the life of Jesus, following much prayerful study and thought. It would be a mistake, however, to conclude that the Trinitarian nature of God is inherently a contradiction. "Persons" (centres of consciousness) and "beings" (entities) are not the same thing, which means a more-than-one-person type of being is entirely *possible* – it is just somewhat mind-bending.

God having three centres of consciousness and yet remaining as a single entity might well be a tough assertion for us to take on board, but it is no more befuddling than some of the claims of quantum mechanics or general relativity. After a 1958 lecture on quantum fields, for instance, Niels Bohr announced to the speaker:

> We are all agreed that your theory is crazy. The question that divides us is whether it is crazy enough to have a chance of being correct.[1]

As we might have guessed, the "crazy" theory being proposed by Wolfgang Pauli (1900–58) in that lecture is now accepted. More than that, it actually forms part of the bedrock of modern physics. Developments like this tell us that highly complex ideas – even those that flirt with paradox – can still be both true and of enormous value.

The biblical concept of the Trinity is indeed a difficult one, and wrapping our brains around it is not straightforward. For Christians, though, this is the idea that agrees best with their experience of God, as well as with Scripture. Theories that seem to reach beyond common sense to explain experienced reality hold no fear for the scientist, however: he or she works with similarly bewildering notions on a daily basis.

Why, apart from the parallels of paradox in faith and science, are we even discussing this? We have wandered into the realm of *theology*, and we appear to be discussing it in technical detail, too. Should this not be the realm of priests and theologians or be confined to the private life of a believer? What possible difference could the doctrine of the Trinity make to a book about *science*?

For now, the key observation is this: the Bible presents God as being *relational* as part of his very essence. God the Father, God the Son, and God the Holy Spirit are all eternal, meaning that they have coexisted in loving relationship forever. Crucially, this relationship must have been present before anything else was created. Before the universe and humanity were made, therefore, there was already love, friendship, loyalty, unity, diversity, trust, and commitment – each of them perfectly enacted. Where were all of these wonderful things? Within God himself.

This is the stage on which we, as human beings, arrive. The Trinity created us to *join in* with this relationship. We were made, uniquely, with the inbuilt capacity to love God – and to do so with the same perfect love that he embodies. We were made with the ability to live out a genuine friendship with God. The Bible, in its opening book Genesis, puts it this way:

> Then God said, "Let us make mankind in our image, in our likeness…"
> So God created mankind in his own image,
> in the image of God he created them;
> male and female he created them.[2]

A human being is therefore an extraordinary thing – Paul says that humanity is God's "masterpiece" – and each one has been given an extraordinary invitation. We, almost unbelievably, are invited into the Trinity relationship. This is evidenced in John's writings, in which he identifies Jesus as being one of the three Persons of the Trinity: God the Son. In his Gospel, for example, John recounts an "intra-Trinitarian" conversation between Jesus and God the Father. On the topic of humankind, the Trinity, and relationship, Jesus prays that:

> all of them may be one, Father, just as you are in me and I am in you.

and that:

> they may be one as we are one – I in them and you in me – so that they may be brought to complete unity.

and, finally, that:

> the love you have for me may be in them and that I myself may be in them.[3]

For Jesus, who prays this on his way to his death, this is the endgame: for people to be brought together into a perfectly loving relationship with him, with the Father, and with the Spirit. It is an invitation that the Bible does not extend to either the angels or the animals, although these two groups can still enjoy and worship God in a more limited fashion. Only human beings, the Scriptures say, are made in the likeness of God. Only they can join the Trinity in perfect love.

The relationship with God that we have been discussing, however, is not the only one that the Bible says we were designed for. Three further bonds are mentioned – all of which flow from a healthy love of the Creator.

First, as we might have deduced from the prayers of Jesus above, we are also made to live with *one another* in unity. Second, we were intended to be at peace with ourselves *internally*, just as God is. Third, we are called to love the creation around us – to treasure *nature*. This final relationship, which often receives less attention than the others, is highlighted early on in Genesis:

> The Lord God took the man and put him in the Garden of Eden to work it and take care of it.[4]

To help him with this, God instructs Adam to give a name to each animal[5] – a detail that can be easily passed over. Yet, as any expectant parent (or designer, or artist, or inventor, or scientist) will know, choosing a name is a precious thing. In the ancient world, names were given even more significance: they conveyed deep information about that person or object.

If we combine, then, the divine directive to "take care of" and "name" nature with the promised "covenant with the stones" mentioned in Job, a picture of developing tenderness between humanity and the world begins to emerge. God made both us and nature with the intention that we would live in harmony.

All in all, then, the Bible describes four human relationships, the first of which sets the tone for the others: God–people, people–people, people–themselves, and people–nature. Each of these was designed by God to be loving. Each was designed to be perfect. This is why we can read: "God saw all that he had made, and it was very good."[6]

Very good, that is, until it all went wrong.

Four Separations

In Chapter 5, we detailed the series of events in the garden of Eden that Christians call "the Fall". We can recap them now: Adam and Eve rejected God by calling both his wisdom and his love into question. They went against his instruction, trusting other influences and temptations more than they were willing to trust God. The biblical term for the rejection of God in any form is "sin".

Sin, according to the Bible, can be either active and deliberate or passive and careless. It is, essentially, any denial of God as he reveals himself or of his values. Going further, the Bible identifies the root of sin as being our desire to exalt ourselves above God. It says we have an unrelenting and woefully mistaken conviction that he cannot be trusted – that we know better than he does.

The effect of such a breakdown in trust on a relationship is disastrous and, in this case, it is fourfold disaster. Francis Schaeffer (1912–84), the esteemed American philosopher, is one of the many to write about the consequences of humanity's decision to turn away from their Creator:

> Another way to look at the results of the Fall is to notice the separations that are caused by sin. First is the great separation, the separation between God and man. It underlies all the other separations, not only in eternity, but right now. Man no longer has the communion with God he was meant to have. Therefore, he cannot fulfil the purpose of his existence.[7]

Schaeffer mentions *other separations*, and he goes on to name them, giving the same list that we looked at in the previous section. The biblical message is this: we rejected God's wonderful invitation to join in with the love of the Trinity and, in doing so, brought about our own punishment. Our own pride has cut us off from God and his qualities, causing pain and hurt between us and him, us and others, and us and ourselves.

Alongside this, as we saw in Chapter 5, God responded to our rejection by bringing about a fundamental change in our bond with nature – a "curse" – manifesting as ignorance and "hard toil". This change is a signpost to us that something has gone desperately wrong. All four relationships are on the rocks. Schaeffer, referencing our ill-fated human determination to "out-God" God, says:

> Man's sin causes all these separations between man and God, man and himself, man and man, and man and nature. The simple fact is that in wanting to be what man as a creature could not be, man lost would he could be.[8]*

And yet, as a Christian, Schaeffer believes deeply that this dreadful situation is not the end of the story. His analysis of the Fall takes a positive turn as he calls on another resounding theme of the Bible – one that we have considered already ourselves in Chapter 5. There is, Schaeffer says, in the middle of all of this mess, still *hope*:

> But there is one thing he did not lose, and that is his mannishness, his being a human being. Man still stands in the image of God – twisted, broken, abnormal, but still the image bearer of God...
> ...Man still has tremendous value.[9]

What, though, is the significance of this value? And how, exactly, does it bring hope?

The Return of the Prodigal

Much of Jesus' teaching during his ministry was given – as we mentioned in Chapter 2 – in the form of analogy or story. Many

---

* Shaeffer's language reads in a gendered way today; it's important to understand that in his time "man" stood for "all humans", without a thought of biasing men over women.

of his stories have broken through into mainstream culture; one of the best known is that of the "Prodigal Son". In it, Jesus speaks of the human condition, describing it as one of self-imposed broken relationships and loss. It is worth running through the main plot points, as they will prove highly relevant to our present study of the biblical big picture.

A man – who is clearly perfectly fit and well – has two sons. The younger of the two asks, rather impertinently, for his inheritance: right now and in cash. Receiving it, this son heads off to waste it on a lavish surface-level existence. Soon, penniless, he is forced to take on a job considered unthinkable to the average Jew: he becomes a swineherd. Thoroughly miserable, and with time to think things through, he realizes his mistake. He wants to go back to the life he had with his father. Knowing that he is overwhelmingly guilty, he prepares himself for a severe telling off and a deserved change in status:

> I will set out and go back to my father and say to him: "Father, I have sinned against heaven and against you. I am no longer worthy to be called your son; make me like one of your hired servants."[10]

What happens next is crucial. As far as the Bible is concerned, Jesus is God himself. And here he is, telling what is effectively the story of humanity. The ending Jesus gives to this story will therefore speak of our own fate: for this is *God telling us about us*.

Will the father (God) accept the returning son (humankind)? Will the son be received back as a servant and lose his sonship forever? Worse still, might he even be divinely obliterated? The father's response in this parable will mirror God's response to anyone who comes to their senses, repents, and turns back to him. For that reason, this might just be the most important story ever told. So how does it end?

> But while he was still a long way off, his father saw him and was filled with compassion for him; he ran to his son, threw his arms around him and kissed him.[11]

The prodigal – wasteful – son is welcomed back with *compassion*. In fact, he is accepted in the most outrageous act of self-abasing love – the head of a household running out to meet a guest in this way was practically shameful.

Is the father, perhaps, unaware of his son's immoral and selfish behaviour? Is that why the welcome is so wonderful? Perhaps questioning all this himself, the son blurts out his rehearsed speech – and this results in an even deeper display of his father's love:

> The son said to him, "Father, I have sinned against heaven and against you. I am no longer worthy to be called your son."
>
> But the father said to his servants, "Quick! Bring the best robe and put it on him. Put a ring on his finger and sandals on his feet. Bring the fattened calf and kill it. Let's have a feast and celebrate. For this son of mine was dead and is alive again; he was lost and is found." So they began to celebrate.[12]

The message of Jesus to the listening crowd is emphatic. Yes, they have rejected him. Yes, they have taken their inheritance and wasted it. Yes, they are guilty. But they are welcome back. They will be forgiven. Those who are desperately *lost* can be *found*; those who are *dead* can be made *alive*.

The spiritual love and spiritual hope that Jesus speaks of in this parable are deeply moving when grasped in full. They moved Job and Asaph and Habakkuk and Paul and John. They moved Grosseteste and Copernicus and Kepler and Faraday and Maxwell.

In the story of the prodigal son, and in many passages elsewhere, the Bible broadcasts the most wonderful of all messages: the broken relationships of the human condition – all four of them – can be fixed by this running Father. One day, it promises, this fixing process will be complete. For now, it reminds us, there is work to be getting on with. And this work, it would seem, will include *science*.

The Ministry of Reconciliation

The apostle Paul was a deep thinker, as were many of his fellow Bible writers. This is important, because when we consider the divine "welcome back" displayed in the story of the prodigal son, it seems, at first, as if there is a glaring hole in the logic.

It may certainly be loving for God to show compassion to a repentant sinner, but is it *fair*? How can a perfect God overlook wrongdoing in this way? Where is the divine justice that is referenced – as we have seen – in so many biblical passages? Paul and his fellow authors wouldn't let an issue like that slide, would they?

It is time now to look at the last piece of our theological puzzle: can

God welcome back even the worst of sinners with an embrace and yet still maintain justice? The biblical answer is a rather emphatic "yes". He can do it, we are told, by lifting the guilt from *our* shoulders and placing it firmly on *his*.

As extraordinary as it may seem, the God revealed in Scripture is prepared to do this. In the person of Jesus, he takes upon himself the sin of humanity and is brutally punished for it in his death on the cross. God becomes the sacrifice for us. He pays our ransom. He "redeems" us.

We can see this promise of justice and liberation in the Bible over and over again. Consider, for example, the words of Job, or those of Isaiah:

I know that my Redeemer lives,
and that in the end he will stand on the earth.[13]

But he was pierced for our transgressions,
he was crushed for our iniquities;
the punishment that brought us peace was on him,
and by his wounds we are healed.[14]

Going even further, the Gospels of Matthew and John both have Jesus himself explaining that he would stand in the place of the sinner and pay the price of their wrongdoing, so that they may go free:

the Son of Man did not come to be served, but to serve, and to give his life as a ransom for many.[15]

I am the good shepherd... I lay down my life for the sheep... no one takes it from me, but I lay it down of my own accord.[16]

In this second statement, Jesus is confirming the voluntary nature of his rescue mission. Divine justice will be upheld. Sin will not go unpunished. By taking our punishment upon himself, Jesus creates a way for us to come back to God without having to face the consequences of his righteous anger at our moral failings.

The teaching that Jesus' death can bring us back to God is sometimes called the doctrine of the "atonement", which is a contraction of "at-one-ment". In other words, his sacrifice means that people and God can be "at one" again. For Paul, a man driven by his heart and his head, this all made sense. God made us and loves us; we turned away and are undeniably guilty; God bears the punishment instead of us; we can return to our Maker with the promise of compassion and peace.

Paul realized that the atonement left room for God to be both merciful and just, and he considered this to be the most profound truth he had ever come across. He said it summed up the "power" and the "wisdom" of God. He became determined to spread the good news of the Jesus who had given his life for all.

Paul, we recall, had encountered this Jesus personally on the road to Damascus, discovering that he had risen from the dead. As a committed scholar, not given to fancy, Paul viewed this resurrection as conclusive *evidence* of both Jesus' deity and of the success of his saving work on the cross. And, unsurprisingly, he wanted everyone else to know it too.

For Paul, spreading the news involved two distinct processes. First, he travelled extensively, preaching about the risen and victorious Jesus Christ across much of the Middle East and even into Europe. Second, he wrote many letters to the newly formed churches that were springing up around the ancient world. In one of these letters – now known as 2 Corinthians – he discusses the atonement, using language that will become very important for us:

> For Christ's love compels us, because we are convinced that one died for all, and therefore all died. And he died for all, that those who live should no longer live for themselves but for him who died for them and was raised again… Therefore, if anyone is in Christ, the new creation has come: the old has gone, the new is here! All this is from God, who reconciled us to himself through Christ and gave us the ministry of reconciliation: that God was reconciling the world to himself in Christ, not counting people's sins against them. And he has committed to us the message of reconciliation. We are therefore Christ's ambassadors, as though God were making his appeal through us. We implore you on Christ's behalf: Be reconciled to God.[17]

In this passage, we see the atonement spelled out clearly – *He died for all* – and we are then led directly to the ultimate purpose of Jesus' life, death, and resurrection. It is, Paul says, all about the healing of relationship.

God, the Trinity, the perfect expression of love, unity, and friendship, is fixing everything that has gone wrong with us and with the world. He is bringing about *reconciliation*. Paul says this message of love and hope *compels* him to share the good news with others.

He has been given, he says, an opportunity to tell sinners that God will not count their *sins against them*. Things need not stay broken: *the new is here*. God, in his mercy, has made a way back. Paul, to his great joy, has been called into this *ministry of reconciliation*, and he *implores* people to investigate the story of Jesus further: *be reconciled to God*.

If the Fall led to four broken relationships, the atonement can lead to four full repairs. The work of Jesus makes it possible for God and people to come back together again. This will then lead to the same for people with themselves, people with each other, and people with nature.

We have seen already, in Chapter 5, that these bonds will only be fully restored at a future time. And yet we also know that the Christian is instructed to use that hope as a motivation for improving them in the present. He or she should work positively to build and grow each of these potentially wonderful relationships, enjoying them as they do so. This, Paul says, is the very purpose of our earthly life, so it is therefore worth repeating it: *be reconciled to God*.

Off Topic, or Not?

We have given over quite a few pages now to biblical theology. Rather than merely referencing the Christian worldview, we have considered the doctrines of the Fall and of the atonement – and the underlying theme of loving reconciliation – in far more detail than one would typically find in a book claiming to be about modern science.

Can this be justified at all? Have we headed off on a tangent that is, if we are honest, somewhat irrelevant? After all, what can the Bible's four separations, four promises of full restoration, and four commands to strive for better in the present actually contribute to the practical, real-world work of today's scientist? In short: what can this theology say that could ever inform our science?

Let us be under no illusion: there are those who would shout loudly (and do) that the answer is a big fat "nothing". Others go even further and say that religious teachings will only ever be opposed to good and productive scientific work. Take the thoughts of Sam Harris, American author and neuroscientist, as an example:

> The maintenance of religious dogma always comes at the expense of science… Iron Age beliefs — about God, the soul, sin, free will, etc. — continue to impede medical research and distort public policy.[18]

If this is true, our consideration of the ministry, death, and resurrection of Jesus is not just a waste of time, it will actually make things worse for the scientist. Biblical thoughts of long-broken and yet still fixable relationships will not be beneficial: they will hold laboratory work back.

Fortunately, the concerns raised by Harris might not be as serious as he thinks. They have not, for example, been borne out in the overall story of Christianity and science so far. Peter Harrison, an Australian historian and former Oxford professor, writes:

> Historians of science have long known that religious factors played a significantly positive role in the emergence and persistence of modern science in the West. Not only were many of the key figures in the rise of science individuals with sincere religious commitments, but the new approaches to nature that they pioneered were underpinned in various ways by religious assumptions.[19]

This second point is of special importance. Sam Harris would have us believe that Christianity necessarily hampers science, but the evidence is against him. It is not even the case that Christianity has been a neutral non-influence. It has, as a faith, *underpinned* some of the most significant scientific work ever carried out. The *Oxford Handbook of Philosophical Theology* points to just some examples:

> Newton embraced a theory of gravitation involving the then-proscribed notion of action at a distance (short-range repulsion in this case) on the basis of his belief in God's omnipresence... Faraday's field theory was connected to his theology of God as creator and sustainer. Maxwell's field equations modelled his views concerning relationships within the Trinity. Further, religion-friendly aspects of contemporary cosmic fine-tuning cases cannot be dismissed as easily as some would like.[20]

The message is clear: when we talk, in a science book, about Christianity and the God revealed through its Scriptures, we are emphatically *not* off topic. On the contrary, it seems that we might be sitting squarely in the middle of it. Science, it would appear, thrives within a Christian culture.

To investigate why that might be, let us begin by summarizing what we have learned from all the stories, people, and passages that we have come across in the previous chapters. Once we have done so, we will be able to ask one of the biggest questions of them all: could the reason for Christianity's great benefit to science be, perhaps, that it is *true*?

Data Analysis

In Chapter 2, we sought to debunk the commonly held view that science only came into being when religion began to die off; that real science is, at the most, a few centuries old. By taking a journey back through time, we found that this was most certainly not the case. Our pursuit of wisdom about nature is as ancient as any of our other tendencies. Human observation and analysis of the world have been there all along. Science and faith have walked together, hand in hand, from the very beginning.

Chapter 3 – via pomegranates and moth larvae – showed that science is hardwired into the human being. The Christian teaching that the Creator of the universe also created our minds and our ability to think gives an explanation for this that cannot be equalled in power by any other. Not only did we read in the Bible that the capability to do science is God-given; we found that we are actively invited, by him, to act on it.

Extending this principle, Chapter 4 discussed the high value that Christianity places on wisdom and on following the evidence wherever it leads. The conversion experience – which holds within it a complete change of worldview – also puts the Christian in an excellent position to be "born again" scientifically. The personal revolution of conversion, as the story of quantum mechanics demonstrated, is excellent preparation indeed for scientific revolution.

In Chapter 5, we addressed the fact that science is not easy. Smooth progress is rare, and real-world lab work is more often characterized by intellectual – sometimes even physical – pain. Despite this, scientists keep going. The deeply human instinct that "things are not right" and the accompanying hope that "things really can be better" carry them forward.

We saw that this is a picture, in miniature, of the Christian view of the human condition. We have fallen away from what was meant to be, but we are given a promise of a fully restored future. In the meantime, we are to work hard, with God's help, for any restoration that can be achieved now. Believing that life is like this on the grandest of scales, as the Christian does, makes real science more bearable and joyful; it provides the faith needed to press on.

The theme of Chapter 6 was that the Christian God brings order from chaos. Individual events may exhibit an apparent randomness, but God's plan is eternal, and he maintains a divine big picture. The struggling Christian can trust this God, even when it seems that there has been a loss of control.

We saw this same tight-knit relationship between randomness and predictability in the hyper-modern understanding of chaos theory, statistical mechanics, quantum mechanics, and even geophysics. God's creation, it seems, shows similarity on all scales. Trillions of unpredictably colliding molecules combine to form well-behaved water; the turmoil of earthquakes and thunderstorms combined to form a safe path for the Israelites.

Far from promoting blind faith, Chapter 7 described a Christianity that has questioning at its very core. Jesus, as presented in the Gospels, asked far more questions than he gave answers. The God of the Bible expects us to have enquiring minds. Often, scientific progress comes as the result of asking a new question, something that Christians should be doing all the time.

Finally, Chapter 8 addressed a topic that some might initially have thought rather unscientific: love. Biblical love, however, is not purely emotion: it is active and committed, treasuring beauty and goodness highly enough to keep going under the harshest of conditions. Love, we are told, carried Jesus to the cross. Just as our selfless love nurtures babies through childhood and into maturity, it also carries young and weak scientific ideas through into adulthood. Love – which the Christian believes has its origin and prototype in God – has long proved essential in science.

These findings strongly suggest that there is some sort of profound resonance between Christianity and science. The principal claims of the Bible about us and our world are echoed in our scientific work time and again. The principal attitudes that God calls Christians to have are those which produce the best scientific results.

Science has experienced some of its biggest leaps forward in Christian environments, with Christians heavily involved, attributing both their motivation and success to their Maker. In even a fairly short survey we have found enough evidence to suggest that the relationship between science and Christianity runs very deep. Before we can declare any bold, overarching conclusion from all this, though, it seems wise to exercise a little caution.

Spurious Correlation?

Tyler Vigen is fascinated by data. He is not a scientist in the professional sense, but he is pursuing wisdom about our world with the same enthusiasm (if not more) than many who are. He could be called, to borrow a religious term, a lay scientist. On his website,[21] he explains his motivation:

> Empirical research is interesting, and I love to wonder about how variables work together… I'm not a math or statistics researcher… but I do have a love for science and discovery and that's all anyone should need.

Once again, interestingly, we find the word *love* popping up in relation to science. Vigen also considers his work to be "fun" and hopes that his project "fosters interest" in anyone who comes across either his online work or his book. So what, exactly, has he been up to?

The World Wide Web has an awful lot of numbers on it. Almost every imaginable type of statistic is stored on it somewhere. What Vigen has done is plough through them all automatically, looking for patterns. Specifically, he is looking for "correlations" – when one set of statistics matches the behaviour of another.

Any match found is then given a score, in the form of a percentage. If the two data sets behave identically, that score will be 100 per cent. Anything higher than 90 per cent would ordinarily draw the attention of a practising scientist; anything higher than 95 per cent, and papers could even be published, claiming one factor is causing the other.

This is all well and good in cases where there is a clear relationship between the factors – comparing height with arm span, or amount of snowfall with snow-shovel sales, for instance – but sometimes we aren't sure whether one thing is related to another, and we need to test for it. Is a 95 per cent score or better always enough to know? Vigen's project – *Spurious Correlations* – would suggest not. He checks for high scores that don't make any real sense, and has already found more than 30,000 of them.

Here's one: the divorce rate in the state of Maine year-on-year seems to follow almost exactly the same pattern as the amount of margarine eaten per US citizen year-on-year. In fact, over the decade from 2000 to 2010, the correlation score between the two was 99.26 per cent – a number almost Nobel Prize-worthy if found in a formal study. Even this, though, can be beaten: the score linking how many lawyers draw a wage in American Samoa each year with the annual rainfall in Wyandot County, Ohio is 99.95 per cent.

We know that these relationships are not *real*; they are just quirks, coincidences. Yes, the scores are high and the data looks impressive on a chart, but there is nothing deeper going on. Anyone campaigning for a national effort to eat less margarine in the hope of improving the quality of marriages in Maine would be considered utterly mad. Vigen's work reminds us of an important principle: there can be matches in data points without there being any relationship at all.

Imagine, however, that a team of scientists had raised a concern about an ingredient in American margarine years ago. Imagine that they had developed a hypothesis: eating too much of it might have a detrimental effect on our mental health. Imagine that they had suggested it could result in bursts of anger, and that these would be worse in colder, more humid climates. Imagine that they suggested the tendency towards violent behaviour accumulated over time. What would we think of the score given above now?

Much would be in place to seriously consider rethinking margarine recipes. Maine is colder and more humid than many other states. Bursts of anger might contribute to fractious relationships. If the effect accumulates over time, this is more likely to affect marriages. Suddenly – and however unlikely we might have thought it at first – we would need to investigate further. We would have to face the possibility that the Franken-marge crisis was real.

Blind Faith?

How is this relevant to our discussion of Christianity and science? Well, the case has been put forward in this book that the former is of great benefit to the latter. Sure enough, we have seen that there are lots of data points that would suggest this is true; each chapter has added more. We must be careful, though, not to jump to conclusions just because there appears to be a match: it could, after all, be spurious.

This time, though, the link should not be dismissed. The resonance we have discussed between Christianity and scientific endeavour is not a fluke. The heliocentric revolution, the fields revolution, the quantum revolution, the statistical revolution: all involved Christians at the very forefront. This could, of course, be a matter of chance – if it were not for a few key truths.

First, the Bible gives careful and reasoned predictions about what our experience of the world will be like. It tells us that the universe was once perfect, and has fallen. It tells us that we have become ignorant of our world, but that the means of becoming reacquainted are deep within us. It tells us that God's creation exhibits both randomness and order. It tells us that we will get answers to our questions, but that these will sometimes be hard won. It tells us that we can see wonder and beauty in nature when we look for it, and that the harder we look the more we will find. The Bible, therefore, has predicted what real, human science will be like: and it is right.

Second, the scientists with Christian faith who have contributed to profound developments in our understanding have repeatedly pointed to their Christianity as being a factor in their work – and, in some cases, the dominating factor. This should not be ignored. It is a major piece of evidence, and it supports the biblical argument above. Knowing God, and seeking to know him better, has advanced science far more successfully than could ever be attributed to chance.

Third, the alternative positions are far from persuasive. As much as some might want to rile against Christian theology and decry it as wholly unacceptable in the laboratory, they are hard pushed to supply any feasible replacement. If there is no God, and our brains are the product of pseudo-directed randomness, how is it that we can trust them? How is it that we are able to deduce the deep mysteries of our cosmos? If we are bent purely on animalistic survival, how is it that we consider it worthy to search for theoretical answers that will have no practical application to life whatsoever – and, even more so, how on earth could we expect to find them?

Attempting to answer these questions without calling on the foundational teachings of Christianity leads to nothing but speculation. The only way that we can do science in a godless universe is to cross our fingers and believe that our brains are capable of it, a belief which cannot be verified, since we would have to use our brains to do so. Ironically, if we throw God out of science, we are left with no other option but to exercise *faith*. This faith is a faith in ourselves, and – because we can never gather any evidence for it – it is, by definition, *blind*.

What is Science for?

The biblical teachings of the creation, the Fall, the atonement, and of future restoration have been the driving force in many of the science stories we have looked at. Even when scientists do not believe them, they still borrow these principles unwittingly. They trust their own brains, they see the beauty in nature, they acknowledge the brokenness of the world, they ask questions about it, they believe that progress is possible, they work to bring it about, and they love doing so. All of these convictions and actions flow naturally from the grand human story presented in the Bible.

If science, then, is an undertaking so powerfully resonant with Christian Scripture, might Christianity also tell us what science is *for*? The answer is yes, and we can go back to Paul to see how.

> For since the creation of the world God's invisible qualities – his eternal power and divine nature – have been clearly seen, being understood from what has been made.[22]

Science, Paul says in effect, is a gift from God. When we carry out scientific work – when we love looking for wisdom about nature – we are seeking to join in, as it were, with the work of our Maker. As we do so, we become able to "see" a little more about how the divine mind works, and this, in turn, can help us to pursue relationship.

Paul was not writing in the context of a battle against atheism, so he is not making the simplistic claim that we can deduce from the universe whether there is a God or not. In fact, he is going much further than that. He says that our study of the world can help us find out what our God is *like*, his *qualities* and *divine nature*. By sharing in – and enjoying – God's understanding and wisdom we can be drawn in closer to him, should we so wish: just as he invited Job, he invites us.

The Trinity, through the sacrifice of Jesus, has made it possible for the four broken relationships of the human condition to be healed, as we have seen. Like the prodigal son, we are welcomed back. We can return home to our God and be forgiven, our punishment paid.

Wonderfully, we can then begin to play our own part in fixing things – with his help. We can use the belief that things will be fully restored one day as a motivation and model for seeking restoration right now. We can work on knowing God better, knowing each other better, knowing ourselves better and knowing nature better, and science can contribute to all of these.

Science, as provided by God, is designed to help heal broken relationships. God has built into us a scientific aptitude, a hope of making progress, and a love for discovery so that we can get on with doing just that. Physics, chemistry, and biology – along with all of their related disciplines – are given to us as a beautiful and powerful gift by a wise and relational God.

What is science *for*? It is for one thing: *reconciliation*. The calling on the scientist – and the calling that should be coming *from* them, too – is a deep one. Be reconciled to nature. Be reconciled to yourself. Be reconciled to other people. *Be reconciled to God.*

10

CROSSING THE ROOM

We are called to live in this world in the light of Christ's example and of the new creation: to seek with all our scientific, technological, medical, financial, social, and personal abilities to remedy some of that brokenness that human sinfulness has caused and continues to cause.

Robert White

In the distance tower still higher peaks which will yield to those who ascend them still wider prospects, and deepen the feeling whose truth is emphasized by every advance in science: that great are the works of the Lord.

J.J. Thomson

At the start of this book, we listened in on several different conversations about science with the intention of then navigating through them – something we likened to crossing a cluttered room. What furniture might we need to be aware of? What potential hazards lay scattered on the floor? Having taken these into account, we planned our course – one which would build the claim that science is a gift from God, designed to bring about reconciliation with nature, other people, ourselves, and God.

Has this resulted in any collisions? Have we trodden on something painful? Have we even, perhaps, arrived at a new doorway? In this final chapter, we shall look once more at Chapter 1's varied attitudes towards science, asking how our intended path through the room worked out. Is there anything valuable to learn about the items we have passed? Was the journey actually worth taking? Have we, ultimately, ended up in a better place?

Science the Spooker

The sharp-eyed reader will have noticed that this was, in fact, the final opinion we heard in Chapter 1 – we will be working through them in reverse order this time around. George Steiner, we recall, said that the "inhuman otherness" of the world around him was deeply disconcerting; he felt alienated by the universe. "Only art", he said, could resolve this problem and bring about any comfort, any reconnection. Given the discussion in the previous chapters, can we now comment on Steiner's thoughts productively?

We have seen that the Bible describes humanity as having fallen into a state of darkened ignorance about nature; that our relationship with it has been damaged as a result of "sin", a turning away from God. The words of Job are highly relevant here: we were intended to have "a covenant with the stones", but instead our experience is one of "painful toil". This is what Steiner was observing: the Fall has led to us finding nature to be somehow "other".

Carrying on with Job, though, we find that this situation does not have to be permanent. We are left with a gift: the ability to re-illuminate the world, to see deeply into it. We read of miners putting an "end to the darkness" by seeking out "nuggets of gold" in the mountain; they bring "hidden things to light". Right from its earliest texts, the Bible makes it clear that our ignorance can be overcome by our God-given ability to be reconciled to nature. This is the gift that makes science possible.

Later, in Jesus' teaching and storytelling, this is explained further: God will always welcome us back. Things that have been "lost" can be "found". The doctrine of the atonement gives us hope of reconciliation in all four relationships. Steiner's "otherness" experience need only be temporary; we are enabled and invited to do something about it by a relational God, working at it with his help.

One day – Steiner's "Sunday" – nature will no longer be alien to us in any way. We will have all wisdom about it. The book of Revelation offers us the following vision of the future:

> [The angel] carried me away in the Spirit to a mountain great and high, and showed me the Holy City, Jerusalem, coming down out of heaven from God. It shone with the glory of God, and its brilliance was like that of a very precious jewel, like a jasper, clear as crystal... The foundations of the city walls were decorated with every kind of precious stone. The first foundation was jasper, the second sapphire, the third agate, the fourth emerald, the fifth

onyx, the sixth ruby, the seventh chrysolite, the eighth beryl, the ninth topaz, the tenth turquoise, the eleventh jacinth, and the twelfth amethyst.[1]

In Job, the human workers were able to see what even the bird of prey couldn't, for they along could dig down into the mountain to discover truths about its foundations that were previously unknown. Here, in Revelation, this process is taken to its final fulfilment: all (twelve implies completeness) of the foundations are fully visible at all times. The vision is, therefore, a powerful symbol: nothing about the creation will be invisible or foreign to us.

What, then, do we have to say to Steiner? Simply this: science really can help with his concerns. Science really can bring us back into relationship with the world around us. He is right to say we are currently living in the "long day's journey of the Saturday", but we shall not remain there forever. The hope of the Sunday to come should inspire us, today, to seek out wisdom where it may be found. Comfort – some of it at least – is available right now.

Before we move on, let us briefly address Steiner's comments about art. If science is primarily concerned with reconciliation, what of the arts? Does the scientist need to dismiss the artistic world as a potential friend or colleague in the walk towards a better day – as a helper in reconnecting to the world around us?

While this is not the subject of this book, the Bible has just as much to say about the positive role of music, song, sculpture, architecture, and more in aiding us to know God and his universe better; there is also great goodness and joy to be had in using his gifts creatively. We are even told that God gives heightened artistic abilities to certain individuals:

Then the Lord said to Moses, "See, I have chosen Bezalel...
and I have filled him with the Spirit of God, with wisdom, with understanding, with knowledge and with all kinds of skills – to make artistic designs."[2]

It is God's intention for us to live in community – to be reconciled to one another – and this will involve the interaction of different gifts, including those of artistic and scientific kinds. Steiner was half-right: art can indeed help us. His mistake, however, was not to credit science with the same. Why, we might ask, didn't he do so?

Science the Odd Family Member

Too often, as we have seen, science is presented as a distant and almost mysterious process carried out by a small number of super-intelligent people behind closed doors. Evidence and data, we are led to believe, are handled with machine-like precision; new facts and theories emerge in pristine condition. Nothing ever goes wrong: scientists know exactly what they are doing, and they march ever onwards doing their odd-and-complicated-but-highly-effective "thing".

In his highly entertaining book, *The Secret Anarchy of Science*, former nuclear physicist and science writer Michael Brooks lays out this idea – which he calls a highly successful "cover-up" – as follows:

> The brand identity of science is reinforced with adjectives such as logical, responsible, trustworthy, predictable, dependable, gentlemanly, straight, boring, unexciting, objective, rational. Not in thrall to passions or emotion. A safe pair of hands. In summary: unhuman.[3]

It is hardly surprising that Steiner, like so many others, thinks of science and scientists as unconnected with everyone else, as unable to offer any comforting reassurance. How can science be expected to speak at all to the human condition if it is *unhuman*?

We know, from the stories we have found, that this *brand identity* of science is almost completely false, something which Brooks also points out. We have seen that scientists love ideas that show even the slightest signs of life, throwing their emotions into working with them, even when the data points the other way; think of Copernicus and Krauss. Scientists do impulsive and "unprofessional" things, like throwing water into electromagnets. They are not some exclusive, untouchable grouping; we have observed three-year-olds and online gamers get in on the action.

It seems that some new marketing needs to be done. Can the understanding of science which has arisen from this book help with this at all?

It would appear so. Science, when seen as a gift from God, is given for the benefit of *everyone*. It is there for the express purpose of rebuilding broken relationships. It is human, it is innate; our questioning, wondering minds are made in the image of God's. If science is part of our humanness, and if it is for all of us, then those involved professionally should seek to be as inclusive as possible; we are all in this *together*. How, in reality, might this be done?

Perhaps an answer can be found in an unexpected place: church history. At times, the Christian church has found itself in a not entirely dissimilar position to the science of today. Priests could be viewed as somehow "other", representative of a complex and mystifying system of truths far too complicated and intricate for the general public. The church had its Scriptures and it studied them behind closed doors, emerging every now and then to pronounce new findings or ideas which the common folk were expected to believe without question – if, that is, they knew what was good for them.

It was all too easy for the dynamic to become one of the clergy doing all of the "difficult" theological work and for the laity to then depend entirely on the church's say-so, since they had no real understanding of their own. Those who had taken holy orders could be thought of as operating on a completely different level to everyone else. In short, the church and its official staff could almost be considered to be – borrowing the language of Brooks again – *unhuman*.

Like the science of today, therefore, the medieval church set-up sometimes alienated the ordinary man or woman on the street. Nowadays, clever use of technical scientific jargon can close down conversation or even enable dishonest pseudo-scientists to exploit the masses – who often feel hopelessly out of their depth. In the past, public ignorance of – or even lack of access to – the Bible left the door open for dishonest pseudo-priests to do the exactly the same with their congregations.

These problems in the church perhaps reached their height towards the end of the Middle Ages. In the fourteenth and fifteenth centuries in Europe, the Bible was only readily available in Latin, a language only useful to the educated minority, and sometimes not even known to the local churchmen. It would be naive to think that some of those employed to look after the Christian welfare of the general population did not take advantage of this situation. After all, they were deemed by the vast majority to be God's representatives, so what they said went. Such power can, sadly, corrupt.

Thankfully, other Christians were sufficiently concerned at all this to seek some sort of change. How could the church be more of a shared community, with all Christians actively involved in it? How could there be more of a functional, genuine relationship between all believers, ordained or not? How could the questioning mind be encouraged, rather than shut down? How could false religious teaching or practices be exposed for what they really were?

One answer stood above all others: translate the Bible into the language of the people, and teach them to read it for themselves. This would empower those who were at risk of being duped or marginalized to advance their own understanding of and involvement in the Christian life. It would promote individual study, open discussion of ideas, and – crucially – personal responsibility for one's own relationship with God.

As a result, the New Testament concept of "the priesthood of *all* believers" began to circulate with far greater emphasis, and became a major part of Christian thought as the Middle Ages drew to a close. One pioneer of the translate-and-teach philosophy was the outstanding scholar at Oxford University at the time, John Wycliffe (1320–84), who made his position very clear:

> Christ and His Apostles taught the people in the language best known to them... the doctrine should not only be in Latin but in the vulgar tongue... The laity ought to understand the faith and, as doctrines of our faith are in the Scriptures, believers should have the Scriptures in a language which they fully understand.[4]

One knock-on effect of all this was a huge surge in adult literacy in Western Europe. This, in turn, paved the way for even those from the humblest of backgrounds to make some sort of impact on the thinking of the day. It helped to bring about a levelling of society which, although still a long way from complete, had never been equalled before, and this took effect both inside and outside the church.

Perhaps, then, science needs a few Wycliffes of its own. Might it benefit from the same sort of translating and teaching model? Is there a way in which professional scientists can be called into question? Can the general public be helped to think, scientifically, for themselves? Can science be re-humanized, somehow? Some brave innovators would say that the answer to all of these questions is yes – and they are, as a result, cracking on with it.

Brady Haran trained as a journalist and is now a film-maker. Like Tyler Vigen (Chapter 9), he is also a "lay scientist", indulging the fascination that we have said is God-given. Using the highly public medium of YouTube, he has made it an aim to destroy the "exclusivity" of science: he interviews professional chemists, physicists, mathematicians, and more, challenging them to explain their work at a level which anyone can understand.

The result is remarkable. Haran takes a wonderful "everyman" approach with him, questioning the scientists further whenever he is not satisfied. It is possible to get some sense of his work from just one conversation with a particle physicist, Dr Clare Burrage:

HARAN: Theory isn't quite matching what happens in reality...

BURRAGE: Right...

HARAN: ... You just invent a particle to paper over the cracks.

BURRAGE: That's basically what we do in physics.

HARAN: That doesn't seem right to me... that seems naughty,
that doesn't seem elegant.[5]

This sample interaction is indicative of Haran's ability to speak for the viewer. He calls professionals to account – not in an aggressive manner, but in a way that is driven by curiosity and fun. In doing so, he draws comments from some of the brightest minds in the world that lay bare the myth of cold, logical science. It is impossible to come away from his various channels still thinking that science is "unhuman". Laughter, honesty, and the reality of scientific struggles all feature regularly.

Seeing science for what it really is – creative and yet imperfect people being *people* – can bring new levels of accessibility and involvement. It will stimulate interest and stop science from being seen as the odd family member. We are arguing that real science is an inherently human activity, just as music or art or sport is. Everyone should be involved.

Most people have a favourite song. Most people have a carefully chosen painting or photograph on a bedroom wall. There is no real reason, Haran and the biblical view of science would argue, why they might not know and love a particular scientific story, theory, or finding too. After all – and as we have discovered in this book – there is plenty of beautiful, surprising, and even funny science to be found out there.

Any increased willingness among professionals – whatever their area of work – to communicate the "humanness" of what they do is a hugely positive step for all of us. Let the artist describe their use of colour to the chemist. Let the chemist explain the origins of colour to the artist. We are all in this, the Bible says, together.

Scientists, then, may have made a mistake in shutting themselves away. Thanks to the work of people like Haran, though, more people will be encouraged to delight in wisdom about nature. And, as they do so, they can be further reconciled to the creation that they are both part of and live in – as well as to their God.

Science the Monster-Maker

Has science been unhelpfully, or even dangerously "meddling with nature"? The unfortunate answer is yes, sometimes it has. We should hardly be surprised by this. The problem of sin is a human problem, and that means (as we now know) that it affects scientists too. Michael Brooks again: "This is science: torment, dreams, visions, restlessness, lying, cheating, despair, brawling, bullying, desperation."[6] To back this up, he recounts story after story of results being faked, good work from talented junior scientists being deliberately rejected, ethics committees being ignored, colleagues being knowingly misrepresented, and so on.

These are not the tales of minor characters, either: Brooks names over twenty Nobel Prize winners in his hall of shame. Scientists do not have a unique right to be trusted just because they are doing "science"; they are as likely to do something morally wrong as anyone else is. Can science – or, more fairly, can scientists – make monsters sometimes? Of course it/they can.

The hole in the ozone layer, caused by chemicals called CFCs, was known about for more than a decade before anyone actually did anything effective about it. The oceans are full of plastic. Feeding cows – which are herbivores – to themselves caused an outbreak of mad cow disease. The irresponsible use of untested pesticides has caused deeply unpleasant illnesses. Weapons and chemicals have been tweaked in the lab again and again in order to cause maximum fear and suffering – napalm being one classic example. Outrageous experimentation on people has occurred at many points in our history – and not just in wartime.

The protest might be made that none of this is really the fault of "science" – even, in fact, that science has been the solution to some of these problems. Science remains, however, a human activity, and can be used for good or evil, responsibly or recklessly. It would be grossly naive, therefore, to think that these monsters do not owe at least part of their existence to the scientific method.

If, however, science were primarily viewed as being reconciliatory and as owned by all of us, together, situations like those above would be far less likely to happen. Why? Because there will be a much greater sense of both purpose and accountability. When the ozone issue became a publicly owned one, for example, the story changed. A series of international councils and regulations sought to phase out CFCs; a full recovery of the ozone layer is now expected in two or three decades.[7]

The belief that science is communal would make resolutions like this more common and it would speed them up. It might even help us avoid problems in the first place. Decisions about whether or not to try out a new process that might go on to have a major impact would be shared with those who are not professional scientists. Scientists would be used to making what they are doing as easy as possible to understand. The involvement of everyone else in the conversation would be a regular priority for them.

Similarly, the Bible and the Christian faith would have huge contributions to make on this front. Particularly on controversial topics, those who know the Bible very well and those who know the science very well (hopefully, there would be many who fall into both categories[8]) could talk positively and productively about the best way forward – with the understanding that they are on the same team and are working for the same thing. Will this project, it would be asked, bring about reconciliation in some way? If so, how? What are the risks that we know about? What do the Scriptures have to say on the matter?

Some might criticize such hope as wholly unrealistic or idealistic. Let us not forget, though, that it is always ideals and dreams that drive real change. Recent evidence would also suggest that we are not actually being overly optimistic.

There are already, for instance, some "green shoots" appearing: initiatives which look rather like the shared human project of science that our biblical narrative calls for. In the UK, the "Responsible Research and Innovation" movement pushes for early, detailed, and two-way public sharing of new science. It has even been adopted into the policy of one of the UK's science funding bodies, the Engineering and Physical Science Research Council.[9]

Does science have the potential to be a monster-maker? Yes. Would that happen in a community that was primarily focused on reconciliation? Not deliberately, certainly – and, with biblical wisdom informing the way this community manages its science, maybe not even accidentally, either.

Science the Spoiler

Keats was repelled by science, as we might recall, because it "unweaves" rainbows: it turns things of beauty and wonder into boring bullet points. However, if science is done properly, just the opposite happens. Instead, it takes things that may well be already wonderful and reveals them to be even more wonderful. It is all a matter of good and loving scientific communication, of science-sharing – and of how the hearer then responds.

For as long as scientists are determined to remain a mystical "priesthood" – operating far off from their congregation, popping up every now and then to pronounce a "fact" – this image of Keats's will have some sort of hold. If, however, the biblical function of science is embraced, it will fall away as a distant memory. How so?

We are reminded that Paul says the world tells us of an imaginative and wise God – of who he is and of how he thinks. As Chapter 8 pointed out – and as Brady Haran's videos let us see for ourselves – this means that those involved in science can really love what they are doing. What science reveals, at times, can be genuinely delightful.

Who would have thought, for example, that the arrangement of the seeds in a pomegranate would give rise to computers being able to check themselves for error? Who would have guessed that a child's riddle about a polar bear holds within it such deep truths about the structure of universal space-time?

When creative and imaginative ideas like these are explained with enthusiasm – and especially when they are told as stories – they can become deeply wonderful things. This is what a modern-day Keats needs.

He or she needs to hear that the same physical phenomena which explain rainbows allow us to send light hundreds of miles through minuscule strands of glass, and that this light carries within it millions of tiny pieces of information which add up to form a photograph of a family member or the voice of a dearly loved friend. He or she needs to be told that different animals can see different colours in a rainbow, including some that we humans cannot ever see. He or she needs to explore the potential for wonder at such news: what could those "colours" even "look" like?

Science is no spoiler – it is a generous gift, by which we can use our amazing minds to find out about the even more creative and magnificent mind of our Creator. Science doesn't spoil beauty; it amplifies it many times. It opens up whole unimagined worlds of potential beauty. Let the scientist never be afraid, or embarrassed, to say this.

Science the Moneymaker

Contrary to common belief, the Bible is not against wealth creation – in fact, it is probably more accurate to say that it is in favour of it – but it has a lot to say about what people should do with wealth. Here is one simple example from the book of Proverbs, describing the impressive "wife of noble character":

> She considers a field and buys it;
> out of her earnings she plants a vineyard.
> She sets about her work vigorously;
> her arms are strong for her tasks.
> She sees that her trading is profitable.[10]

The Bible does express serious concern, however, at any form of social injustice, something which, sadly, often accompanies the accumulation of money. James, the brother of Jesus, reminds us that those in society who are most vulnerable should be cared for:

> Religion that God our Father accepts as pure and faultless is this:
> to look after orphans and widows.[11]

What of science and money, though? Does the biblical narrative of the gift and the invitation have anything to say here?

Currently, there is a science-money problem. Research-funding in many countries depends on how many, how regularly, and in which journals science papers are being published, skewing what actually happens in the laboratory.

A priority list of "top" journals arises, the upper echelons of which carry more "prestige" than others. All too easily, the lab's priority becomes the mere production of any new piece of work and having it featured in a prestigious journal – at the expense of finding a valuable new connection with or in our world.

Similarly, if the funding model values quantity of output, it is easiest to take an existing paper and modify that experiment ever so slightly. This tiny tweak allows the work to be considered "original" and off it goes, added to a journal that hardly anyone will read. Nothing new of any note is gained, and imaginative scientific "free play" is limited – almost to the point at which it hardly exists.

We can contrast this situation with the words of Max Planck, the man who accidentally initiated the quantum revolution by "playing around" with maths:

Scientific discovery and scientific knowledge have been achieved only by those who have gone in pursuit of it without any practical purpose whatsoever in view.[12]

Clearly, we need funding models that let scientists off the leash. If God has given us this hardwired, highly creative gift, we should not then restrain those who want to use it. Obviously, the dangers of sin in the monster-making section still need to be taken into account, but money should not be holding us back from seeking deeper wisdom about nature.

Other restraints on imaginative exploration of nature can arise from the worthy practice of "peer review", which requires all scientific publications and all proposals for funding new research to pass a specific test before they get a green light. The papers or plans are written down and reviewed anonymously by experts in the field. This is, usually, a highly ethical and helpful system, and it is right that the scientific community works for quality and efficiency in this way.

But peer review does bring problems. Imagine, for instance, an entirely new or challenging idea emerging, one that calls into question the current way of thinking in a given area. This idea will only ever see the light of day if it is approved by people who support that current thinking; they would have to give the thumbs up to something that threatened to overturn and replace their own deeply held scientific beliefs.

Also, with the cult of "expertise" embedded right at the heart of the professional science model, how can the process ever allow room for science to be a shared or communal activity? Requiring particular "standards" for publication might sometimes work against good ideas – especially if they originated from outside the traditional scientific workforce.

Finally, there is always the factor of a limited money-pot. If there is not enough to go around, what might happen to the work of junior scientists if it has to be reviewed by their seniors, who need funds just as badly? Thinking through these questions – which are both practical and deeply ethical – would be one way of working out a response to a simple but transformational biblical encouragement: "And let us consider how we may spur one another on towards love and good deeds."[13]

Once we recall that doing science is one way that people both *love* and do *good deeds*, this idea from the New Testament book Hebrews looks like a serious command to turn peer review from a conservative force into a creative one.

Science the Saviour

Can science really save us all, as Pandit Nehru had suggested? Can it change the world, as Royal DSM claimed? The message of our study is both a "yes" and a "no".

The renowned Harvard historian and economist David Landes (1924–2013) undertook a challenging task indeed in writing *The Wealth and Poverty of Nations*: he sought to explain why it is that there are rich and poor countries in the world. Summarizing the great developments in the quality of life in Europe following the Industrial Revolution, he says:

> Advances in medicine and hygiene exemplify a much larger phenomenon: the gains from the application of knowledge and science to technology. These give us reason to be hopeful about the problems that cloud present and future.[14]

Landes points out that both germ theory (which came too late for Semmelweis) and automated cotton production (echoes of Jacquard) had radically positive impacts on life expectancy and health. Here we see "pure" science and "hands-on" technology working together for the benefit of the human race. Landes uses this interplay as a basis for saying that we can be positive about the future, too.

Sometimes it is a new abstract idea which triggers fresh progress; sometimes it is an innovative machine. A science built around relationship – one in which shared "togetherness" is treasured – would result in those who are primarily engaged in theoretical work communicating regularly and clearly with those more focused on practical work. Doing reconciliatory science can indeed change the world for the better, and it should. Crucially, though, it cannot *save* it.

This is because the fundamental problem with humanity, as far as the Bible is concerned, is not a lack of scientific knowledge. It is not even a lack of wisdom about nature. It is a moral failing – sin – and the broken bond with our Creator that arises as a result.

The story of the prodigal son and the offered gift of atonement, however, tell us that it really is true that "things can be better", since God invites us back into relationship. The science he has given to us can bring about wonderful improvements in our quality of life as we become reacquainted and reconnected with the world around us, with ourselves, and with each other. It can also offer us glimpses of the mind of God himself. The decision to pursue reconciliation with him further, however, is an individual one.

Biblically, it is not really the "world", as a single entity, that is saved by anyone or anything – not by God, not by "religion", not by "science". Instead, each person is called to make a choice whether or not to follow Jesus. Those that do are called to live as a loving community, working hard to bring about as much good as they can: and this includes doing good science.

This science, though, does not "save the world". Our true hope, the Bible says, is found in the final and complete restoration of relationship which is made possible by the life, death, and resurrection of Jesus. If there is to be a saviour, then, it is not science. It is Jesus.

Science, Faith, and Hard Words

Once again, we have found ourselves in theological waters, but, hopefully, they no longer feel quite as strange. The histories and the stories of Christianity and science are deeply intertwined and, from the journey we have mapped out in this book, we know that it is actually more unusual to think of the two as separate than as together.

As much as some would have us believe that faith and science are enemies and that the new "modern" scientific worldview must be allowed to win out, we have seen that this arises from a false view of their relationship.

One sad outcome of this mistaken assertion is that "faith" and "science" are seen, by so many, as "hard words" – distant, confusing, and uncomfortable. Both are actually intended to be the opposite: welcoming, joyful, and reconciliatory.

The Bible sees science as a gift from God, and he invites us to pursue it. By doing so, we discover new wisdom about nature, about ourselves, and – if we are prepared to look deeply – even about him. Relationships that have been damaged can begin to be restored. Ignorance can be overcome. Hope replaces despair; love replaces fear.

How can we sum up what we have found in the preceding pages? What has been the result of crossing the room? We have been on a grand journey, encountering story after story; so what, at the end of it all, can we say we have learned?

First, that science is all about reconciliation. It brings people together, it mends relationships, and it restores our understanding of nature, of each other and – should we want it to – God.

Second, that science should be shared. It is a deeply human activity, one that is hardwired into all of us. There should be no hidden exclusivity, no deliberate alienation through the use of technical language, and no elitist grouping that keeps wisdom about nature away from others. Science brings joy, and joy should be communicated as widely as possible.

Third, that the professional scientific community should work alongside others. Since science is human, many can contribute valuably, even if they have no formal training. Journalists, gamers, and even toddlers have done exactly that. Public conversation and ownership can help science maintain a conscience. Input from outside might even improve scientific decision-making.

Fourth, that the faith community should celebrate and enjoy science, not fear it. Science is a God-given pursuit, and he blesses it. Just as a church might commission, in public prayer, a teenager heading overseas with a missionary organization, let them do the same with someone leaving to study biology at university, for both are working for reconciliation. Both, if they are committed to the biblical narrative, can seek to bring future goodness into the present. Both are doing God's work and using his gifts.

In its first book, Genesis, we read one of the Bible's many creation stories. We find the Trinitarian, relational God speaking into a dark world, making it knowable and visible for the very first time: "let there be light".

We can use this same language to encourage people who might have, up until now, considered themselves on different sides of all sorts of divides: let there be reconciliation; let there be togetherness; let there be a sharing of wonder and joy and curiosity and discovery; let there be a love of wisdom about nature. We can say all of this – and much, much more – in just four words:

"LET THERE BE **SCIENCE**."

NOTES

FOREWORD

1. John 3:16.
2. Psalm 139:14.
3. Confessions 1.1.
4. 1 Corinthians 2:9.
5. 1 Corinthians 12:12.

1. TURNING THE LIGHT ON

1. www.theguardian.com/commentisfree/andrewbrown/2010/jun/29/richard-dawkins-atheism-schools (accessed 29 March 2016).
2. "Professor Says Science Rules Out Belief in God", *Electronic Telegraph*, 11 September 1996.
3. Ravi Zacharias, *Beyond Opinion* (Thomas Nelson, 2008), p. 23.
4. www.theblaze.com/stories/2013/11/22/evolution-and-creationism-concerns-rage-in-texas-textbook-debate (accessed 29 March 2016).
5. "The Making of Optical Glass in India", *Proceedings of the National Institute of Sciences in India* 27 (1961), pp. 564–65.
6. www.sciencecanchangetheworld.org/home.html%20-%20nav (accessed 29 March 2016).
7. www.londonstockexchange.com/exchange/prices-and-markets/stocks/indices/constituents-indices.html?index=UKX (accessed 29 March 2016).
8. www.scientificamerican.com/article/cost-to-develop-new-pharmaceutical-drug-now-exceeds-2-5b (accessed 29 March 2016).
9. Chancellor of the Duchy of Lancaster, *Realising Our Potential: A Strategy for Science, Engineering and Technology*, Cm2250 (London: HMSO, 1993).
10. www.ifs.org.uk/conferences/kcl_mo2013.pdf (accessed 29 March 2016).
11. *Breaking the Magician's Code: Magic's Biggest Secrets Finally Revealed* (Nash Entertainment, 1997–2002).
12. www.youtube.com/watch?v=OD8n0ONBTls (accessed 29 March 2016).

13. www.sandiegouniontribune.com/uniontrib/20050714/news_1mi14jenkins. html (accessed 29 March 2016).

14. Jean-Pierre Fillard, *Is Man to Survive Science* (World Scientific Publishing Co., 2015).

15. *Jurassic Park*, Steven Spielberg (Universal, 1993).

16. www.dailyscript.com/scripts/jurassicpark_script_final_12_92.html (accessed 29 March 2016).

17. www.bbc.co.uk/programmes/b006qj9z (accessed 29 March 2016).

18. www.bbc.co.uk/programmes/b02lwy59 (accessed 29 March 2016).

19. Bill Bryson, *A Short History of Nearly Everything* (Doubleday, 2003), p. 23.

20. George Steiner, *Real Presences* (Faber & Faber, 1989).

2. AN ANCIENT STORY

1. Alfred North Whitehead, *Process and Reality* (The Free Press, 1978; originally published 1929), p. 39.

2. Galileo, *Two New Sciences*, trans. Henry Crew and Alfonso de Salvio (MacMillan, 1914), pp. 107–108.

3. Walter Kaufmann, *The Faith of a Heretic* (Princeton University Press, 2015; originally published 1961), p. 76.

4. David Hume, *Enquiry Concerning Human Understanding* (1748), 12.34.

5. Proverbs 18:17.

6. Brian Clegg, *Roger Bacon: The First Scientist* (Constable, 2003), preface.

7. "Responsive Gels Formed by the Spontaneous Self-Assembly of Peptides into Polymeric Beta-Sheet Tapes", *Nature* 386 (1997), pp. 259–62.

8. Bede, *On the Nature of Things and On Times*, trans. Calvin Kendall and Faith Wallis (Liverpool University Press, 2010).

9. Gregory of Nyssa, *On the Soul and the Resurrection*, trans. C.P. Roth (St Vladimir's Seminary Press, 1993).

10. Mark 7:14–19.

11. Ben Goldacre, *Bad Science* (Harper Perennial, 2009).

12. Daniel 1:12–14.

13. Judges 6:36–40.

14. Isaiah 28:27–28.

15. Cf. Rome, Bibl. Vat., MS Chigi A.VIII. 245, f. 16va.

3. A GIFT AND AN INVITATION

1. Audio Recording for Chimp Island, Alasdair Gillies, Blair Drummond Safari Park.

2. James Essinger, *Jacquard's Web* (Oxford University Press, 2004).

3. Thomas L. Heath, *The Thirteen Books of Euclid's Elements*, 3 volumes, 2nd edition (Dover Publications, 1956; originally published 1925).

4. See, for example, Florence P. Lewis (Jan. 1920), "History of the Parallel Postulate", *The American Mathematical Monthly* 27, no. 1 (1920), pp. 16–23.

5. Johannes Kepler, *The Six-Cornered Snowflake*, trans. Colin Hardie (Clarendon Press, 1966).

6. "Hales Solves Oldest Problem in Discrete Geometry", *The University Record* (University of Michigan), 16 September 1998.

7. For a comprehensive account of Jacquard, Babbage and more, see Essinger, *Jacquard's Web*.

8. R.W. Hamming, "Error detecting and error correcting codes", *Bell System Technical Journal* 29, no. 2 (1950), pp. 147–60.

9. For a more thorough and mathematical description of this process, see Jordan Ellenberg, *How Not to be Wrong* (Allen Lane, 2014).

10. Job 28:1–11.

11. Romans 1:20 (NLT).

12. Job 38:16–30.

13. Johannes Kepler, *Optics*, trans. William H. Donahue (Green Lion Press, 2000), p. 15.

4. REVOLUTIONS

1. *Monty Python and the Holy Grail*, dir. Terry Gilliam and Terry Jones (Michael White Productions, 1975).

2. E.T. Whittaker, *A History of the Theories of Aether and Electricity*, Vol. 1 (Nelson, 1951).

3. Albert Einstein, *Out of My Later Years* (Citadel Press, 1956).

4. Einstein, *Out of My Later Years*.

5. *The Science Book* (Dorling Kindersley, 2014), p. 185.

6. Anton Z. Capri, *Quips, Quotes, and Quanta: An Anecdotal History of Physics* (World Scientific, 2007), p. 93.

7. E.N. da C. Andrade, *Rutherford and the Nature of the Atom* (Doubleday, 1964), p. 111.

8. Alan P. Lightman, *The Discoveries: Great Breakthroughs in Twentieth-Century Science, Including the Original Papers* (Alfred A. Knopf Canada, 2005), p. 8.

9. Werner Heisenberg, *Physics and Beyond* (Harper and Row, 1971), p. 206.

10. Stephen Hawking (ed.), *A Stubbornly Persistent Illusion: The Essential Scientific Works of Albert Einstein* (Running Press, 2007), p. 310.

11. Richard Dawkins, *The Selfish Gene*, 2nd edition (Oxford University Press, 1989), p. 198.

12. Richard Dawkins, *The God Delusion* (Bantam Press, 2006), p. 28.

13. Revelation 22:8–9.

14. Job 31:26–28.

15. Proverbs 8:22–31.

16. Proverbs 8:1–11.

17. Psalm 73:1–14.

18. Psalm 73:16–28.

19. Acts 9:1–2.

20. Acts 26:2–15.

21. Acts 26:19–20.

22. Acts 26:24.

23. Acts 26:25.

24. Romans 12:1.

25. Ephesians 4:22–23.

26. C.S. Lewis, *Surprised by Joy* (Harvest, 1966).

27. B. Jones, *The Life and Letters of Faraday: Volume II* (Longmans, Green and Co., 1870), p. 384.

28. Draft of a reply to an invitation to join the Victoria Institute (1875), in Jones, *Life and Letters of Faraday II*, p. 404.

29. Max Planck, *Scientific Autobiography and Other Papers*, trans. Frank Gaynor (Philosophical Library, 1949), p. 184.

30. Ulrich Hildebrand, "Das Universum – Hinweis auf Gott?", *Ethos (die Zeitschrift für die ganze Familie)*, no. 10 (October 1988).

5. PAIN, SUFFERING, AND HOPE

1. See www.cracked.com/article_18501_7-incredible-scientific-innovations-held-back-by-petty-feuds.html for more information on Semmelweis and Meigs (accessed 29 March 2016).

2. George Steiner, *Real Presences* (Faber & Faber, 1989).

3. Isaac Newton, *Philosophiæ Naturalis Principia Mathematica*, viewable online at www.ia802706.us.archive.org/0/items/newtonspmathema00newtrich/newtonspmathema00newtrich.pdf (accessed 29 March 2016).

4. www.newtonproject.sussex.ac.uk/view/texts/normalized/THEM00258 (accessed 29 March 2016).

5. Eddington actually did not get very good results from his experiment, and his decision to back Einstein was as much due to gut instinct and politicism as anything else. For more on this, see Michael Brooks, *The Secret Anarchy of Science* (Profile, 2011).

6. Lee Smolin, *The Trouble with Physics* (Penguin, 2008).

7. www.theguardian.com/commentisfree/2013/may/30/will-smith-new-york-magazine-interview (accessed 13 June 2016).

8. Brian Greene, *The Fabric of the Cosmos* (Penguin, 2004), p. 329.

9. www.pbs.org/wgbh/nova/physics/conversation-with-brian-greene.html (accessed 29 March 2016).

10. Smolin, *The Trouble with Physics*, p. xiv.

11. www.motls.blogspot.co.uk/2004/10/lee-smolin-trouble-with-physics-review.html (accessed 29 March 2016).

12. www.arxiv.org/pdf/hep-th/0206135v1.pdf (accessed 29 March 2016).

13. For examples of this, see www.online.itp.ucsb.edu/online/resident/johnson2 (accessed 29 March 2016).

14. Genesis 3:17–18.

15. Genesis 3:15.

16. Job 7:1–3.

17. Job 19:25–27.

18. Job 5:21–23.

19. Isaiah 65:22–25.

20. Romans 8:18–24.

21. Revelation 22:1–3.

22. 2 Peter 1:3–11.

23. John 16:33.

6. ORDER FROM CHAOS

1. Tom Stoppard, *Rosencrantz and Guildenstern are Dead* (Faber and Faber, 1967).

2. www.statweb.stanford.edu/~susan/papers/headswithJ.pdf (accessed 29 March 2016).

3. Pierre-Simon Laplace, *A Philosophical Essay on Probabilities*, trans. F.W. Truscott and F.L. Emory (Dover Publications, 1951), p. 4.

4. www.nature.com/nnano/journal/v7/n5/full/nnano.2012.42.html (accessed 29 March 2016).

5. www.hyperphysics.phy-astr.gsu.edu/hbase/solids/squid2.html#c1 (accessed 29 March 2016).

6. R.M. May, "Simple Mathematical Models with Very Complicated Dynamics", *Nature* 261, no. 5560 (1976), pp. 459–67.

7. Edward N. Lorenz, "Deterministic Nonperiodic Flow", *Journal of the Atmospheric Sciences* 20, no. 2 (1963), pp. 130–41.

8. Christopher M. Danforth, "Chaos in an Atmosphere Hanging on a Wall", Mathematics of Planet Earth (April 2013), www.mpe.dimacs.rutgers.edu/2013/03/17/chaos-in-an-atmosphere-hanging-on-a-wall (accessed 29 March 2016).

9. Stoppard, *Rosencrantz and Guildenstern are Dead*.

10. Job 31:2–8.

11. Job 12:15.

12. Job 9:5–6.

13. Job 14:18–19.

14. Job 9:16–17.

15. Psalm 121:3–4.

16. Job 38:2–3.

17. Job 38:22–27.

18. Robert S. White, *Who Is To Blame?* (Monarch, 2014), p. 10.

19. Isaiah 54:10.

20. Habakkuk 3:17–18.

21. Psalm 77:15–20a.

7. QUESTIONS AND ANSWERS

1. www.highlightskids.com/science-experiment/make-pinhole-camera (accessed 29 March 2016).

2. Joseph Needham, *Science and Civilization in China: Volume 4, Physics and Physical Technology, Part 1, Physics* (Caves Books, 1986).

3. Alistair Cameron Crombie, *Science, Optics, and Music in Medieval and Early Modern Thought* (Hambledon Press, 1990), p. 211.

4. Eric Renner, *Pinhole Photography: From Historic Technique to Digital Application* (Focal Press, 2009), p. 226.

5. www.amorebeautifulquestion.com (accessed 29 March 2016).

6. *LIFE*, 2 May 1955, p. 64.

7. Alberto Martinez, *Science Secrets: The Truth about Darwin's Finches, Einstein's Wife and Other Myths* (University of Pittsburgh Press, 2011).

8. Abraham Pais, *Subtle is the Lord: The Science and the Life of Albert Einstein* (Oxford University Press, 1982), p. 131.

9. www.bbc.co.uk/news/health-26189827 (accessed 29 March 2016).

10. www.nobelprize.org/nobel_prizes/physics/laureates/2010/geim_lecture.pdf (accessed 29 March 2016).

11. www.nature.com/scitable/topicpage/protein-structure-14122136 (accessed 29 March 2016).

12. Readers can have a go themselves at www.fold.it/portal (accessed 29 March 2016).

13. Firas Khatib et al., "Crystal Structure of a Monomeric Retroviral Protease Solved by Protein Folding Game Players", *Nature Structural and Molecular Biology* 18, no. 10 (2011), pp. 1175–78.

14. www.independent.co.uk/voices/interview-messing-with-the-messiah-william-leith-meets-a-n-wilson-the-man-of-letters-who-upset-the-1551051.html (accessed 29 March 2016).

15. www.amazingbibletimeline.com/bible_questions/q10_bible_facts_statistics (accessed 29 March 2016).

16. Genesis 3:8–9.

17. Habakkuk 1:2–3.

18. Habakkuk 1:5–6.

19. Habakkuk 3:18.

20. Colossians 1:15–17.

21. Matthew 8:26.

22. Matthew 9:4.

23. Matthew 9:28.

24. Matthew 14:31.

25. Matthew 16:21.

26. Matthew 19:17.

27. John 8:46.

28. John 14:9.

29. Mark 8:29.

30. www.dailymail.co.uk/news/article-1169145/Religion-hatred-Why-longer-cowed-secular-zealots.html (accessed 29 March 2016).

8. LOVE

1. "The Lights of Zetar", *Star Trek: The Original Series*, Gene Roddenberry (NBC, 1969).

2. 1 John 4:8.

3. John 15:12–13.

4. 1 Corinthians 13:4–8.

5. 1 John 3:16, 17.

6. Proverbs 3:11 and Hebrews 12:5–6.

7. 1 Corinthians 13:12–13.

8. Ralph Waldo Emerson, *Society & Solitude & Other Essays* (Forgotten Books, 2013), pp. 142–43.

9. Copernicus, *De revolutionibus orbium coelestium* (1543).

10. The authors are grateful to Professor Owen Gingerich of Harvard University for his personal correspondence on this matter.

11. www.sciencecanchangetheworld.org/meet-more-scientists.html (accessed 30 March 2016).

12. www.nytimes.com/2008/06/01/opinion/01greene.html?_r=0 (accessed 30 March 2016).

13. www.parade.com/37704/parade/12-inside-a-great-mind/ (accessed 30 March 2016).

14. www.thehindu.com/todays-paper/tp-features/tp-sundaymagazine/all-in-the-brain/article1449254.ece (accessed 30 March 2016).

15. www.hmimmigration.com/news/big-data-bad-prophets-and-brian-cox-an-interview-with-tim-harford#.VvuYNdIrKUk (accessed 30 March 2016).

16. Lawrence M. Kraus, *The Physics of Star Trek*, new edition (Flamingo, 2010).

17. Lawrence M. Kraus, *A Universe from Nothing* (Simon & Schuster, 2012).

18. www.map.gsfc.nasa.gov/universe/uni_shape.html.

19. Paul Feyerabend, *Against Method* (Verso, 1975), p. 116.

20. Louis E. Van Norman, *Poland: The Knight Among Nations* (Fleming H. Revell, 1907), p. 290.

9. RECONCILIATION

1. Freeman Dyson, "Innovation in Physics", *Scientific American* 199, no. 3 (September 1958), pp. 74–82.

2. Genesis 1:26–27.

3. John 17:20–25.

4. Genesis 2:15.

5. Genesis 2:19.

6. Genesis 1:31.

7. Francis Schaeffer, *Genesis in Space and Time* (InterVarsity Press, 1972), p. 98.

8. Schaeffer, *Genesis in Space and Time*, p. 100.

9. Schaeffer, *Genesis in Space and Time*, pp. 100–101.

10. Luke 15:18–19.

11. Luke 15:20.

12. Luke 15:21–24.

13. Job 19:25.

14. Isaiah 53:5.

15. Matthew 20:28.

16. John 10:11, 15, 18.

17. 2 Corinthians 5:14–19.

18. www.huffingtonpost.com/sam-harris/science-must-destroy-reli_b_13153.html (accessed 30 March 2016).

19. www.abc.net.au/religion/articles/2012/05/08/3498202.htm (accessed 30 March 2016).

20. Thomas P. Flint and Michael Rea (eds), *The Oxford Handbook of Philosophical Theology* (Oxford University Press, 2009), p. 65.

21. www.tylervigen.com/spurious-correlations (accessed 30 March 2016).

22. Romans 1:20.

10. CROSSING THE ROOM

1. Revelation 21:10–20.

2. Exodus 31:2–4.

3. Michael Brooks, *The Secret Anarchy of Science* (Profile, 2011), p. 2.

4. www.christianhistoryinstitute.org/magazine/article/archives-why-wycliffe-translated.

5. www.youtube.com/watch?v=7VxcTXud-Tg (accessed 30 March 2016).

6. Brooks, *The Secret Anarchy of Science*, p. 260.

7. www.epa.gov/ozone-layer-protection/current-state-ozone-layer (accessed 30 March 2016).

8. See, for example, David Wilkinson, *When I Pray, What Does God Do?* (Monarch, 2015), Tom McLeish, *Faith and Wisdom in Science* (Oxford University Press, 2014), Francis Collins, *The Language of God* (Simon & Schuster, 2008), and John Polkinghorne, *Quantum Physics and Theology* (Yale University Press, 2008). All are written by scientific experts who are biblical Christians; all deal with the direct and practical interaction of Christianity and science.

9. www.epsrc.ac.uk/research/framework (accessed 30 March 2016).

10. Proverbs 31:16–18.

11. James 1:27.

12. Max Planck, *Where is Science Going?* (Ox Bow Press, 1981), p. 138.

13. Hebrews 10:24.

14. David Landes, *The Wealth and Poverty of Nations* (W.W. Norton, 1998), p. xix.

INDEX